The Old Neighborhood

To Monument Circle

Dogpatch

Margaret McFarland School #4

Heaven

Churchman Avenue

Timmy's House

Bethel

Raymond Street

To Manual High

Jimmy's House Street

Wade

Creek

Avenue

Ronnie's House

Bradbury St.

Walker   Street

Hobart Bridge

Jimmy's House

Bean

Author's Homes

The Outhouse

Old Swimming Hole

Sarah Shank Golf Course

Tommy's House

To Bosma's Dairy Bar

Gullible's Travels

Stories from the Journey of a Lifetime

Gullible's Travels

Steven Clark Goad

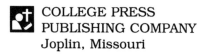
COLLEGE PRESS
PUBLISHING COMPANY
Joplin, Missouri

Library of Congress Cataloging-in-Publication Data

Goad, Steven Clark.
    Gullible's travels: stories from the journey of a lifetime /
Steven Clark Goad.
        p.   cm.
    ISBN 0-89900-797-X
    1. Christian life—Churches of Christ authors.   2. Christian
life—Humor.   3. Goad, Steven Clark.   I. Title
BV4501.2.G587 1997
286.6'092—dc21
    [B]   97-31581
                                                                              CIP

Acknowledgments

First of all I would like to thank my parents for giving me a healthy environment in which to mature. We were daily arranging for precious memories . . . in advance.

To my in-laws I am indebted for their patience as we bounced stories (literally) off their ears and then requested critiques. Being well read, they were gentle and graciously invaluable in making suggestions. Thanks to friends who screened several of the stories over the period when the book was being written. Kisses for wife Laura for all her time in preliminary editing.

I am indebted to a few close preacher friends who have encouraged me in my writing over the years in special ways: Jim Bill McInteer, Joe R. Barnett, Dr. F. Furman Kearley, Charles Hodge, Wayne Frump, Curtis Dickinson, Ray Downen (the dear man who literally sent me cash and typewriter ribbon during my downtime wanderings in the desert), Edward Fudge, the late Reuel Lemmons, Sam Stone, Dr. Steven Lemley, elder Leland Lutz and others. I would be remiss if I did not mention my beloved elders Jere Allen, Oscar Osburn and Jim Wood for tolerating the writing style of this author all these years as I edited our challenging church bulletin, yet still encouraging me in the ministry of the gospel of Christ.

Especially am I thankful to my "old neighborhood" buddy, Jimmy Van Busum, with whom I have reconnected, for his applause and helpful critique. What a thrill to have master illustrator Gary Royse able to work his visual talents at the last minute in order to provide magical art.

Last but not least is my beloved editor and friend, John Hunter — a more patient encourager one could not possibly find. He and his staff at College Press have diligently and beautifully made this process of publishing yet one more volume for human history a blessed experience. May all our efforts be for the glory of our heavenly Father in gratitude for His marvelous grace through Christ our Savior.

Steven Clark Goad

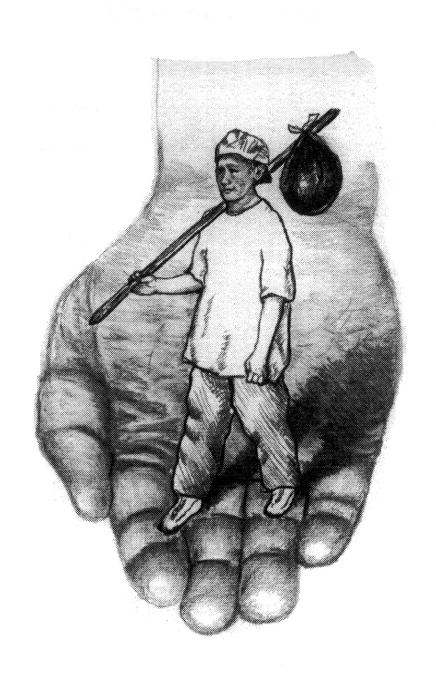

Table of Contents

Preface

Yogi Berra said, "You can observe a lot by watching." I am profoundly indebted to Steven Clark Goad for allowing me to relive my life through his. Every anecdote in his life belongs to mine! God knew what He was doing when He created man. The more time changes, the more we remain the same.

This book is a masterpiece. Goad is a storyteller, a wordsmith, an authentic human being. He sees with his eyes, ears, memory, head and soul. He plays a "tap dance" upon our hearts. He is so honest, naïve, and sometimes downright funny. He exposes his life, peccadilloes, conscience and spirit. What can be a catastrophe is turned into a triumph. As Yogi Berra said, "They said it couldn't be done, but that doesn't always work."

In his nostalgia, he is so wise, so practical. He pulls us back to our roots — family, church, innocence, fears, choices, blunders, yet without braggadocio or fawning. He laughs with and at himself. He makes us laugh; he makes us cry, for there is very little difference between the two.

Goad dares us to find ourselves in his memories, and he calls us to be brutally honest with ourselves. In remembering our youth, he challenges us to mature as adults. As far as I am concerned, he has touched all the bases; he hit a home run! Thank you, Goad, for a job well done.

As Yogi Berra said, "When you come to a fork in the road — take it."

Charles B. Hodge, Jr.

Introduction

A simpleminded person will believe just about anything he is told. Ignorance isn't an easy thing to live with. I remember when I got my first bicycle, some big boy in the neighborhood whose name was Dickey convinced me that I had to change the air in my tires each week or they would rot. Can you imagine how foolish even a little boy can feel when he finally discovers he's been the brunt of someone else's twisted sense of humor?

Don't believe everything you read in the paper and only half of what you see. Don't believe everything you hear on radio or television or from politicians before election time (and after). Being gullible is a tragic waste of time and mental powers. It is a wise person who will weigh what he hears and reads and observes, discarding the useless. It's the business the Bible refers to as separating the chaff from the wheat.

Have you ever been around someone who would try anything once? It's frightening when you think about it. I had a
boyhood friend who couldn't resist a dare. He was, on reflection, one of the craziest guys I have ever known. I thought he
was brave at the time. He would attempt practically anything
his "friends" challenged him to do. So one day we "de-
double-dog-dared" him to do something extremely dangerous.
He almost died trying to please his playmates. Poor Timmy.
We quit daring him after that.

It is a wise person who learns to believe only those things
which are logically reasonable. There is simply too much that
gullible people believe which is simply unreasonable. So I've
been toying for years with the notion of writing a book about
this struggle, which is, in fact, the human predicament: A
book which deals with the gullibility of otherwise normal people trying to cope in a pluralistic society where few absolutes
are nailed down and in which there is little on which to hang
their hopes and dreams. And so, with apologies to Jonathan
Swift, I present to you this string of pearls that chronicle the
"Gullible's Travels" of myself and others as we attempt to
make some reasonable sense of this present chaos called life.

Won't you come along with me as I take this nostalgic
journey? Live again with me these stories of triumph and
tragedy, of inspiration and desperation. Some of the episodes
are obviously autobiographical. Some are testimonies to the
wonder of relationships, as mentors and loved ones are eulo-
gized. Stories were always precious to me, especially at bedtime when Mother would read to me before tucking me in.
Why not keep this story book beside your bed next to your
glass of water? Read one or two tales before retiring and enjoy
the pleasure of going to sleep with a peaceful heart and a
smile on your face.

Chapter One

Beginning the Journey

"Your Choice, Stevie!"

Growing up in central Indiana had its moments of pleasure and pain. On one particularly humid summer day, I had the opportunity to experience both within the span of a few hours. And it was bearable simply because I had someone to share the pain with me. But allow me to begin at the beginning.

It is cathartic confessing one's sins for the whole world to know. But, it is a real and present risk when we choose to confess the sins of others. So, I am in danger here of enraging my partner in crime, for I do not know how to confess my sin without also confessing hers. It's like the lady who responded to the invitation at church one day for prayers, but first she wanted to confess how rotten everyone was at church for not giving her the attention she felt she deserved.

The younger one is, the less guilty he is, right? So my disclaimer is that I was about 4 years old and my sister, Jackie, was 7 or so. This little episode in my life could be called "The Case of the Purloined Toothpaste" because that is exactly what had happened. And if I must say, on reflection, my sister was wise in the ways of the world beyond her years.

Dad, being a good Scotsman, was very frugal and not one to waste his resources. He and Mother could stretch a penny farther than a rubber band. When available, Dad would buy groceries and other household necessities by the bulk. He was way ahead in his thinking for this was long before the "Price Club" idea came along. Dad had purchased a "case" of toothpaste. I don't remember the brand name, and maybe that is unimportant anyway, but I do recall Jackie had a lot of toothpaste and I wondered where she had gotten it. She drafted me to be her accomplice in the dastardly deed. We meandered up and down the streets in our neighborhood selling these tubes of toothpaste for a nickel apiece. Some neighbors were such good customers that they bought several tubes.

It was hot that day as I recall. After covering two streets, my beloved and beneficent sister took us to the corner store and bought us each a popsicle. Ah, it was the good life for a lad in the late '40s. I wasn't worried about Korea or inflation or the cold war. I didn't even fear being kidnapped or molested by some pervert. All I was thinking of was having such a wonderful sister who was so self-sacrificing and who treated her little brother to a free popsicle. It surely couldn't get any better than this.

After consuming the cold treat we headed back to the sweat shop. We finished the rest of the streets and ended up with quite a haul of change. We had done a master job of marketing a product that most everyone used. We were proud of ourselves. Jackie complimented me on doing such a good job of helping by holding the box of toothpaste while she made her presentations. When we got home, we sat down on the porch and exulted in our fortune. Jackie, being the brains of the operation, decided to divvy up the wealth. I had no idea that we had taken something that wasn't ours to sell and sold it for less than it cost dad.

Another "sweet" thing my beloved sister did that day was to allow me to pick what money I wanted. As I recall, all of the money was in nickels and dimes. Having that open-handed spirit of benevolence, Sis held up a nickel and a dime, one in each hand. Then she asked the stupidest question I had ever heard in my life. I actually felt sorry for her for being so dumb. I almost told her it wasn't fair. She asked, "Now, Stevie, you can pick which coins you want. You can have the big ones, or you can have the little ones." Wow! What an offer. Being the astute economic genius that I was, I chose the BIG coins, of course. Jackie stifled a smile. And I was oblivious.

There was a pound of flesh to be paid by each of us for what we did that day. It was the day I began to take spankings in dead earnest for what they were intended to produce. I can't remember being whipped until this day. But I recall Jackie and me tearfully promising never to do such a "wicked" deed again. Had I been able to hire an advocate for myself, I could have pled innocence. I could have, and rightfully so, pled ignorance. For my choice of the BIG coins alone proved that. But, alas, there was a lesson for the ages in the punishment my sister and I received. We learned that it is never right to take what belongs to someone else and use it for one's own selfish gain.

It was the same day we got our first television set. I still remember the first program I watched. It was Groucho Marx and "You Bet Your Life." There was a bearded man on the program who was 100 years old. How I can recall such vivid details of so long ago is hard to fathom. With our new TV one would think it was one of the grandest days of my young life, but it was a tough day for two little thieves. Dad did his best to whip the devil out of us. And we were both grateful for his forgiveness as he reaffirmed his love a few hours later. And I thank God for my first employer, sister Jackie, who has since more than made up for the dimes she snaked from her little brother on that fateful day in the summer of '48.

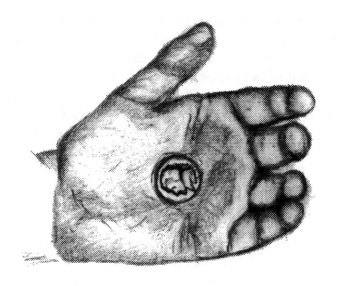

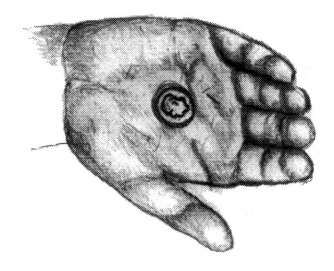

In the Closet

Children are innocent. That is why our Lord tells us bigger folk to become like little children. Kids are cruel, often because they are transparent. They frequently blurt out exactly what they are thinking. Some kid in an elevator asks his mother, "Mom, why is that lady so fat?" Or a little girl announces to her parents that "those hypocrites" from the church are at the door.

We grown-ups have learned all sorts of techniques to keep from allowing people to know what we really think. We wear our masks and facades so cleverly that we are actually able to fool most of the people most of the time. To be totally transparent is to risk exposure. So we hide behind our manufactured personas and pretend to be what we are not and make believe we are nobler than we really are. No wonder Jesus told Nicodemus, "You must be born again."

Since there has been so much devilish behavior in me from my earliest memories, it is difficult for me to admit that once I was innocent and trusting. I actually believed what people taught me and obeyed what I understood the Bible to be teaching me. So I actually did pray in my closet for a week or two, until my mother found me there one day. "Stevie, what are you doing?" She should have known without asking. I mean, she was the one who taught me the most about Jesus and obedience. "I'm praying."

She invited me out of the closet and onto the bed for a heart to heart chat. I told her that I had read in my Bible that Jesus said a person should pray in his closet. And if Jesus said it, I believed it and would do it. Of course, in my formative years I had no idea what "praying in the closet" really meant. The context, on reflection from my present vantage point as a minister of the word, is telling us that public displays of holiness are not what God has in mind for us. If we pray to be seen of men, that is all the reward we shall receive. We discover genuine, heartfelt prayer is a very private matter. And as a kid, I was honoring that truth. I was being as private as I could be, by praying in my closet.

Sadly, I wish I could call back that kind of childlike obedience. I wish I could have the heart of a child instead of analyzing everything to death. The word of God is simpler than we make it out to be. Sure, some things are difficult to understand, but the great and cardinal truths of Holy Writ are within the grasp of even a child's mind. There was room for criticism of my literal application of private prayer, but I certainly didn't violate the principle Jesus taught by going into my little closet and getting on my knees before I said, "Now I lay me down to sleep . . . "

Can we learn from the heart of a child? Do we really understand what our Lord meant when He said, "Allow the little children to come unto me, for of such is the kingdom of heaven"? One thing I remember about being a kid is that my best friends might have made me mad on any given day, but next day they were still my best friends. Grown-ups don't behave that way. They hold grudges. They have long memories. They say their prayers with language that is sanctimonious and sometimes use Elizabethan English to sound more pious, and simultaneously hold harbored hatreds and latent lusts. They engage in affectations to solicit the awe of their auditors, yet displease God in the very act.

Childlike faith is a marvelous thing. All of us need it. When my father asked me to jump into his arms from atop our roof (since foolishness is also bound up in the heart of a child, I was on the roof pretending to be Superman and was literally about to jump [fly] to the ground with a bath towel tied around my neck), I did so without even thinking. It never occurred to me that he might drop me. I never thought he might be fooling me and would step back just the moment I jumped and let me hit the ground and then laugh at me. I had complete trust in my father. And that is the kind of trust we must have in our Heavenly Father as well. That's the kind of faith Jesus had in mind when he taught us to believe without doubting. And it's just the sort of faith that might even drive an adult from his elevated perch at the church house to his own secret "prayer closet" some day.

That Nickel Coke

When does a moral code of ethics kick in for a kid? It may be different for each of us, but I remember to this day the moment in time when I began to understand what guilt was all about. It has haunted me for decades. In the back of my mind has always been the gnawing realization that I had taken something which did not belong to me. Every time I see one of those old-fashioned soda counters I am reminded of the day I stole a nickel coke.

My family was visiting Dad's mother and father in Gamaliel, Kentucky. I must have been five years old. My father and I were in the "big city" of Thompkinsville, for some reason, without my sister and mother. Dad had to go into a dry goods store and left me to enjoy whatever a nickel could buy at the drug store. Back then a nickel could go a lot farther than it will today. Anyway, I looked at the various candies available. Gum. Ice cream. Cheap toys. It must have been hot, for under normal circumstances I would have opted for ice cream over a soda pop any day, especially if it were pineapple sherbet or cherry vanilla. My thirst must have overpowered me. I ordered a Coke.

Coca-Cola was still being served in those pretty green bottles that looked like bowling pins. On reflection, I guess they don't really look like bowling pins, but they did to me at the time. It must have been an entire six ounces of the "real thing" one could fetch for a mere five cents. So there I sat, precariously, on that red, round stool that twirled and twirled. At least it twirled when I was sitting on it. The lady behind the counter was busy with other customers and didn't seem to pay much attention to a little squirt like me. So I coughed in my hand like Mother used to do when she needed assistance from some clerk.

"Yes, Sonny, may I help you?" she asked, as if she were doing me a favor. "I'd like a bottle of Coke, please," I said in my most gentlemanly manner. She rolled her eyes and brought me the Coke with the cap still on it. At least it was cold. It sorta made me mad, if a five-year-old boy can be mad at the rudeness of adults. I had to wait several minutes and cough twice more to get her attention the second time. "What do you want now?" she bellowed. "Could you please take the cap off for me?" She grabbed the Coke bottle and huffed down to the opener and then put it back on the counter with a loud smack. I was not a happy camper.

If I could justify what I did, I might suggest that she had it coming. She deserved to have that soda pop purloined because of her behavior. I was a paying customer with money in hand. As a matter of fact, I had laid the nickel on top of the counter so she could see I was flush. She should have realized that customers deserve better treatment than she had shown me.

Sin doesn't just happen all at once. It creeps up on us unawares. I slowly drank down my Coke and must have thought of how nasty the lady behind the counter really was. The grocery checker at Krogers didn't treat me like that. She even winked at me and ran her hand through my hair. But not this mean old hag. The more I drank, the madder I got. I didn't plan it. I didn't premeditate it . . . not for long at least. I swigged on the Coke a few more times until the bottle was empty. The nickel lay right where I had put it. Hey, if the wicked witch behind the counter didn't see that I had paid good money for my drink, it wasn't my fault. Besides, I wanted to leave and go find Dad.

I did one more twirl on the seat, unstuck myself from the red plastic cover, slid down and started to walk away. I looked back at the nickel. Then, I looked at the lady who was way down at the end of the counter looking in the other direction. I glanced at the door and then again at the nickel. I reached up, took the nickel in my hand and headed for the exit. Nobody said anything. No one cried, "Stop, thief!" I had gotten by with it. Stealing was easy.

It could have led to a life of crime. But somehow, God got a lot of mileage out of that five-cent piece. Its memory has laid heavily on my mind for forty-seven years. If I could go back to the same store, I would be happy to give them back their nickel. I might even give them a dime. "Behold, your sins will find you out!" To this day I prefer Pepsi!

Chapter Two

Juvenile Journeys

Bottle Cap Corsage

Parents are marvelous creations of God — or they ought to be. Mine were. They went out of their way to give us more than they had when they were children. And in their giving to my sister and me, they gave much more than just "things." Kids, then and today, need more *presence* than *presents*. So the greatest gifts of all had to do with things spiritual. We were given the gift of faith by being able to grow up in a Christian home. That faith led us to an "in the days of your youth" acceptance of Christ as Savior. I'm sad today for the children who are part of such dysfunctional home lives that the concept of "mother and father" has just about lost its meaning. Even the very definition of marriage is being challenged.

Kids, in their innocence and at those moments when they

are not totally selfish, which are not very often, attempt to give back to loving parents. This I tried to do for my folks as I was growing up. Usually I needed the urging of a thoughtful schoolteacher or Bible class teacher who would guide my unskilled little hands in the making of some work of art, some arts and crafts piece that would become an artifact of great importance to doting parents who were charmed by such evidence of juvenile devotion. These *objets d'art* would take on various forms: paperweights made of glass coasters and plaster of Paris with school pictures peering up out of the shiny side, various expressionistic creations made with finger paints, homemade greeting cards, figures made of pipe cleaners and toothpicks, ad nauseam.

Mom's dresser drawers became a treasure trove of just such items of love. Those drawers literally became an archaeological dig that uncovered the history of the Goad children. Occasionally, while I was looking for stamps or gum or ice cream money for the Good Humor man, I would run across an artifact or two. After Mother died, we were cleaning out her belongings and attempting to salvage items that could be given to those who had need. I found the silver dollar collection she had kept in cold cream jars. They were made of genuine silver and many were very old and in almost mint condition. On my birthdays Mother would fix my favorite cake, angel food, and then hide a silver dollar in that hollow spot in the middle. I found drawings I had done in pencil. One of sister Jackie's first attempts at sewing was discovered.

It isn't an easy task cleaning out the "things" that were near and dear to a loved one. Dad must have had a much harder time of it than we children did. But for us, it was a time of letting go. Emotionally, it was more important to us than the funeral or the graveside service. The more I dug, the more I was impressed with how very much she loved her children. I uncovered some touching poetry she had written over the years, poetry about my sister and me and Dad. But the thing that touched my heart the most during that "dig" through Mother's dresser that day, was the find at the very bottom of the last drawer we surveyed. Seeing it rushed me backward an entire decade in time as though I had been suddenly forced into a time machine left at the setting of my sixth year of life. It was the flattened and lifeless corsage I had made for her from aluminum milk bottle caps. My first official gift to Mother.

It was about Christmas time when I made that simple gift, and even though we didn't choose to celebrate Christmas at our house when I was growing up, I had made a red, green, gold and silver corsage for Mother as a "Christmas" present. I know you must be wondering why a Christian home wouldn't celebrate the birth of Christ. Actually, we did celebrate Christ's birth, but not the way you might think, so it really is another story in itself. Anyway, my first grade teacher had talked and guided us all through the making of these colorful metal corsages.

Back then, milk was delivered to our home in bottles covered with aluminum caps. The caps were usually plain in appearance. But during the holiday season, some of the milk companies would provide colorful caps on the tops of the milk bottles. I had collected all four colors for my corsage for Mother. It consisted of yarn of uneven lengths with knots tied at the ends. Around these knots we kids wrapped half a bottle cap until it was in the shape of a bell. The knot held the cap in place. After making about eight such flowers, two of each color, we would tie the yarn strings together and put a bow to hide the place where we had gathered them. Voilà! It was a corsage of colorful aluminum "flowers" that looked more like bells than anything else. Mrs. Gettings (that was the teacher's name who helped me make my corsage) calmed our concerns when one kid in class, who was used to stirring the behavioral pot so to speak, actually said, "Hey, Mrs. Spagettings, these here ain't no flowers. Them's bells." (He never could pronounce her name correctly for some reason.) She soothed his excited concerns by saying, "Yes, Billy. This is a corsage of bells, Christmas bells." Billy was dumbstruck, which was quite a rarity for him.

Anyway, when I brought my gift home to Mom, my father had just presented her with a new wool coat. She was so happy over that coat and made out like it was made of spun gold or something even more valuable. So, I felt a bit ashamed of my humble gift, thinking it wasn't much to be giving her after all she had done for me over the years. But by observing her reaction, you would have thought I had given her the most expensive gift in all of the world. "Oh, Stevie, it is gorgeous!" she exclaimed. "Where did you buy it?" I didn't know Mom knew anything about psychology. Of course, I didn't know anything about it either at that moment, so I responded as though she were serious. "Mom, I made it in class! I didn't buy it. I made it from bottle caps," I explained, as if she couldn't see that for herself. She went on and on about how it looked so professionally done and that she would wear it with her new coat to church the very next Sunday. And she did, in spite of the fact that it was a "Christmas" present. I was prouder than a peacock with a new dye job.

The bells weren't bells anymore. They were flattened out, along with the ribbon that held the yarn together. But seeing that smashed corsage of yesteryear brought tears to my eyes. Tears that acknowledged precious memories of parental love and of feeble expressions of affection from little children's hands. She probably would not have sold that little bottle cap corsage for all the gold in Fort Knox. Seeing it lying there safely tucked away in her bottom dresser drawer made me realize how much she had the love of her children tucked away in her heart when she crossed over to the other side.

She was the kind of mother who at the dinner table gave me a chicken leg and ate the back herself. If there was an extra piece of pie she somehow never seemed to want it. "Go ahead, Stevie, you can have the last piece." Her love sat up at nights while I was trembling with chills and fever. I still can hear those muffled prayers she would say at my bedside. She was the mother who was told that after her life threatening delivery of my older sister that she must not risk childbirth again. Yet she wanted a son so badly for Dad, to carry on the Goad name and all, that she eagerly risked her life to have me. She was the brave one, who, one evening in our basement while ironing my school clothes, tried to teach me about the birds and the bees. My innocent response for clarification, "Dinnercourse?", set us both to laughing until our sides ached. I had no idea what she was giggling about, but it was so infectious I couldn't help myself. It still hurts thinking about it.

Those red and green bottle caps were a legacy of love. They reminded me of how marvelous God's design really is as He thought of the concept of family. Mother and father and siblings. How magnificent. How delightful. What a perfect hothouse environment for little ones to grow up in. Yes, I know, Winston Churchill would not approve of the ending of that last sentence, not with *two* prepositions. So I shall end this bit of, admittedly, rambling rhetoric about things too dear to explain, avoiding the violation of any more such rules of grammar. I look forward to reunion day with Mother. Will there be any silver or golden bells up there? I wonder.

On Defending One's Honor

Doesn't the title sound noble? Maybe it's my way of rationalizing what I did one hot summer day in Beech Grove, Indiana. It was muggy. I had just mowed a lawn, one of my week-end jobs. It wasn't the best time to be messin' with the skinny kid on Wade Street. I was in no mood to be harassed.

Maybe I was eleven at the time. I had been brought up in the church. I knew several Scriptures by memory. I had memorized many of the Old Testament Psalms. I could even quote Scriptures for the plan of salvation, and this was even before I had decided to become a parson. Yes, I even knew that Jesus said when someone hits you on one cheek you are to turn the other one to him. But that had to be one of the hardest requests of our Lord in all of the Bible to practice successfully. Besides, I had a few mentors and idols who had taught me otherwise. One was a preacher.

He looked so professorial in his glasses with no rims. Just glass. That's all there was to his spectacles. He had some wire running to them from his ears. I liked him. He was my first impression of what a minister of the word ought to look like and be. One day after services, he was standing on the steps of the church house greeting everyone as they were leaving. Some visitor got into a heated argument with this preacher and became downright belligerent. The man got right in the face of the dear brother. At some point, the parson took off his glasses, handed them to his wife, removed his jacket and unbuttoned his sleeves. The offending party quickly changed his demeanor and said, "I thought you were a Bible believer who was supposed to turn the other cheek." To this our beloved preacher replied, "I'll lay down my Bible long enough to whip your _ _ _!" (He used a colorful term that often refers to a donkey.) This occasion took everyone by surprise and left an indelible mark upon my youthful psyche.

The other fellow I looked up to was a big, gentle man. He was the candy man at church, always giving treats to the kids. Everyone called him brother Billy. He had a lisp and a slight stutter. The combination of the lisp and stutter made him sound silly, sorta like he was using a clown's voice. So, as you might guess, a few unthinking folks made fun of him.

One day some kids in the neighborhood of the church were having fun at this man's expense. He told the kids to go away. A father of one of the kids was nearby and thought the poor man had said something bad to his son. So he came over and started an altercation with brother Billy. He pushed him. Then he shoved him real hard. Brother Billy shouted loudly, "L-l-l-leeave me a-l-l-lone or elth!" That is when the mean father hit brother Billy. Brother Billy just stood there and started to cry. The man thought he was pretty tough, so he hit Billy again. Suddenly brother Billy quit crying. His personality seemed to change right before my eyes. It was like an Incredible Hulk transformation. He stood to his full six feet four inch height, grabbed the man and literally picked him up off the ground. He slammed him into a wall. To make a long story short, the man ended up begging for mercy.

I relate these two accounts, both of which I had witnessed, to justify my behavior which followed days later. Scottie Jackson was sort of a neighborhood bully. He was bigger than I. He seemed to like me, but some days he would pick on me. I got tired of it, but being his junior and all, I let Master Jackson get by with it. Frankly, I was afraid to defend myself. But one day, one muggy, humid, hot, sweltering, Indiana summer day, he made a big mistake. In fun, he threw an egg at me. It may have been the best thing he ever did for me. I had a reputation of being one who would run from a fight. This day, that reputation would change for good.

I don't know if Scottie Jackson knew the egg was rotten or not. But it was. And it broke all over my cheek and neck. It smelled to high heaven. And I got mad. I got fightin' mad. I forgot about Sunday School. I forgot the 23rd Psalm. I even forgot that my Lord told me to turn the other cheek in such encounters. And I lit into Master Jackson with all the energy my 100 pound frame could muster. From that day forward, you would think I was the boy's best friend. He treated me like I was king of the hill. And I relished in my new found glory.

It's wrong to pick fights. But did you ever notice that the Lord didn't tell us what to do after we turned the other cheek and they hit us again? Did He? Okay, so it's pugnacious theology at best, but I still think my Lord allows us poor ones who are picked on from time to time to defend ourselves. Amen?

My Dad

I didn't know I could write at the time. I still doubt, as you might imagine, in spite of my glibness. I remember in high school struggling with the simplest of essays. They surely didn't come easily for me. Later it occurred to me that one must be "inspired" to write material that is interesting to others, and for those school essays I just wasn't inspired.

Though only ten years old at the time, I was definitely inspired on one particular occasion. The **Indianapolis Times**, a now defunct Scripps-Howard newspaper, had a contest inviting school children to write about why their fathers were the best fathers in the world. That contest was an easy assignment for me because I actually did have the best father in all of the world and wouldn't have to fake it. So, I took the challenge and entered.

As I recall, I sat down at my desk and wrote out my essay in pencil on lined paper. I can't remember what all I said about dad that caught the judges' attention. Some day I want to go back and see if I can find a copy of the paper in which my essay was published. Anyway, I won the contest. Of the 1,000 plus entries, my bragging on father was chosen as the winning essay.

What I won brings a smile to my face even as I recall it. They gave me a case of motor oil, free tickets for two to see Disney's "Song of the South," and a free pizza. Dad was glad for the motor oil. I was hoping for something more on the order of a kid type prize. But it was the movie and the pizza that made me feel proud of being a Goad and being able to have such a wonderful dad.

We bonded during that time together. We had bonded on many previous occasions, but this bond was sort of like super glue for us. I don't recall how Dad expressed his gratitude at my bragging on him in the writing contest, but I am sure he must have been proud. We enjoyed the movie and especially the pizza. We ordered everything on it except anchovies. I don't think I can recall a time in my life when I enjoyed my father's company more.

My dad was from the old school. Stiff upper lip. Men don't cry. The first time I saw him shed a tear was at his father's funeral. Grandpa Goad was in his mid-seventies when he died of a heart attack. I thank the Lord that at this writing my father is still with us, although I have trekked home on about three occasions to say my last goodbyes. But after prayers and medical attention, Dad seemed like one of those Timex watches. He just keeps on ticking. The plastic valve he has in his heart helps a bit. The leg he almost lost to cancer still enables him to be up and about at eighty-two.

My pappy, as we playfully call him from time to time, taught me how to play gin rummy. He was the best in Indianapolis and I can whip him. He taught me how to shoot pool. He was one of the best hustlers in the Circle City and I still can't whip him. He taught me how to play checkers. He was the checker champion in Monroe County, Kentucky and I have never been able to beat him in checkers. And people wonder why I don't take up chess. He "taught" me how to swim by throwing me out of a boat into Dale Hollow Lake in Kentucky. He taught me not to sass my mother. He taught me never to start a fight, but coached me on how to end one if it sought me out.

Dad taught me to wait until the adults got their food before I got mine (a tradition I've noticed has been reversed of recent days, especially at church potlucks). He taught me not to talk during church and to brush my teeth and to take a good bath at least once a week and not to mention the flies when we ate at the relatives while visiting in Kentucky. He even taught me that drinking out of a gourd scoop from a communal water bucket wouldn't kill me. And it didn't. He taught me how to be wise as a serpent and harmless as a dove.

My pop taught me how to throw a ball and catch and run bases. He taught me how to shoot baskets and how to guard others who wanted to. Dad taught me how to like soup beans and cornbread when I'd rather have had steak and ice cream. He taught me how to discipline my children and how to love my wife. The parenting instruction I got was by observation. He taught me impartiality toward siblings.

One night when I was sick with a high fever, Dad stayed up all evening to sit by my bed. He called Doctor West, our family doctor, who made house calls. He mopped my head through my delirium. And when my fever broke and I asked for ice cream, he put on his coat and went out in the rain in the middle of the early morning and found a store still open. Dad rescued my bike from some bully boys who had put it in a tree and then he put the fear of God in all four of them.

I could write a book about what my father means to me and all that he did for me. But the greatest thing he ever did for me, and that any father could ever do for a son, is to see that I was introduced to the Heavenly Father. And as I think of my aged father, I understand why Yahweh chose to identify Himself as our Father.

Body Empathy

We were playing softball at Gloria's house because she had a bigger yard than anyone else. We used stakes in the ground as our bases. Dumb! I mean, how stupid can kids get? No wonder Scripture says "foolishness is bound up in the heart of a child." We never thought about what would happen if someone impaled himself upon one of those stakes, or, if someone fell face first on one and gouged out an eye. So there we were, hitting softballs and running toward wooden, splintery stakes jutting up out of the ground. I guess the safety factor was in our inability to hit many balls. So, only a few of us were in danger of harm. Sadly, I was one of them.

Smack. I hit at least a double, and if I ran hard enough it might even become a triple. So, off I went as fast as my short legs could carry me. I was pretty fast for my ripe old age of 10 and rounded first stake by barely touching it with my heel. It was then I had to decide whether I would go for the triple. "Go for it," I thought, so I poured on the speed. I must have hit that stake with my right big toe at full gallop. My world, for the next few weeks, would not be the same. The pain was intense. It seemed to worsen as the evening wore on. Labor pains and childbirth surely couldn't compare with the agony I was experiencing. The hurting pulsated in deep and unremitting throbs with every heartbeat.

Right after it happened, my playmates ran to my rescue, to sympathize with me. No matter what they said or did to help, I couldn't help but cry. I hated to cry, especially in front of girls. But I let loose a flood of tears that should have helped, but didn't. The pain was there, and it wasn't going away, and cry as I may, there was nothing I could do about it.

My 13-year-old sister got a lot of mileage out of my agony. She actually thought I was faking the extent of my injury. She sort of smirked and chided me for being such a sissy. I wanted to get back at her, but I was unable. And her giggling at my retelling of the story to Mom and Dad only added to my distress. She later felt sorry for me when she learned that I had severely broken my toe, a glaring crack right down the middle of it, that even we could see on the X-ray. Next day she apologized. Even the apology didn't help. The pain was so severe, I couldn't even walk. The doctor prescribed a metal plate for one of my shoes that had to be worn for three months. I wasn't supposed to bend my toe. I limped for weeks afterwards.

Guess what I thought about when I broke my toe? Was my mind on what Mother was fixing for supper? Do you suppose I was thinking of my math homework or whether or not my hair was combed sufficiently to impress the girls? Was I concerned with whether or not I would get the 3-speed bike for my birthday that I had so clearly hinted for in front of Dad? Nope. Was I thinking of what I would do with my life vocationally or whether or not the kids in my block had been sufficiently evangelized? No. All I could think about at that moment in time was *big toe*. I couldn't have cared less whether my teeth were brushed or how long it had been since my Saturday evening bath. The only thing my body was at that moment, and for several days afterward, was right large toe. And I am not exaggerating when I say "large" toe.

Shouldn't our relationships with each other in the body of Christ be similar to my relationship with my toe that dreadful day when play time turned into a nightmare for the Goad boy? It is not an accident that the family of God is called the *body* of Christ. Scripture tells us that we are individual members of the body, just as our eyes, hands, arms, mouths, ears and big toes are members of our physical bodies. Our intimacy with one another, as fellow body members, ought to bring out the best in sympathetic response from all of the other body parts when one in particular is hurting. Our proximity should cause immediate empathy when a body member has been wounded by sin or other matters that might crush him and break his spirits.

Have we learned to both relish in the joy of others and feel their pain when they hurt? Are we genuinely a body of individual members that rush to the immediate aid of one who is limping because of severe spiritual or physical trauma in his life? After the cards are sent and the prayers are offered and the ministering is done, do we still limp with them until the healing is completed? Shouldn't we? Mustn't we?

The Whippin' I Didn't Deserve

It was fun growing up in central Indiana back in the '40s and '50s. Maybe I am remembering from a child's point of view, but things seemed simpler then. The line between right and wrong wasn't so blurred. We knew what our folks expected of us and we knew what we could expect from our folks. Those were the days of Lucy and Ricky Ricardo and Jim and Betty Anderson. It seemed Father really did know best. Well, most of the time.

My father was a stern disciplinarian. He provided the discipline and I provided the stern. Mother was a softy. If ever I got a spanking from her, all I had to do was cry like I was dying and she would let up. But not Dad. If I had it coming, I might as well stand there and take it, because Dad was unrelenting when he thought I had done wrong or disobeyed him. He felt that a kid could take a lickin' and keep on tickin'. And I'm living proof that he was right.

There was only one time that I can recall when I was whipped for something I didn't do wrong. (I've apologized to my kids for whipping them a few times when they didn't have it coming.) My whipping was actually for something my dad may have done wrong, though I am surely not his judge.

One of Dad's jobs when I was growing up was as a milk salesman. He didn't have a milk route. He would drive in a company car and call on people and try to get them to have Banquet milk delivered to their houses. I thought it was a neat job. He sold Oscar Robertson's family milk. He and his partner dressed in business suits and wore hats. They looked like detectives or FBI men. There was a sort of mystique about him driving around in that dark blue car, as if he were doing undercover work.

Anyway, Dad would take samples of milk from the company cooler and give those samples to potential customers. It was a way of saying, "Ma'am, why don't you try our product. I think you'll like it. If so, we'd love to have your business." And it worked. But some days, Dad would have a bottle or two of milk left over and was closer to home than to the milk company, so he would just bring the milk home with him. He didn't do this often, but on one occasion our family was in the middle of building a house and we were living in a tiny trailer with a little ice box. He brought home a bottle of milk. I never thought of it as stealing, and I suppose he never did either.

The next day our milkman came to deliver our milk and asked how much we needed. I said, "Mr. Barker, we don't need any milk today because Dad brought some home from the company." Mr. Barker was a prince of a man. He was like the family doctor and minister rolled into one. He wasn't just our milkman, he was a family friend. He thought the world of my family, and especially my father. I didn't realize what I had done until that evening.

When Dad came home from work, my sister and I were sitting at the table eating cereal. He asked, "Did Mr. Barker leave any milk?" My poor sister, not knowing what was about to transpire, answered, "No, Dad, Stevie told him you brought some home yesterday from the company." You could have heard a pin drop. That's when Dad took me into the bedroom and administered the only whippin' I didn't deserve, and it hurt worse than any I had ever had before. It probably hurt more because I deserved all those other spankings.

My father made a mistake that day that all fathers make at one time or another; he punished me without thinking. He spanked me in a fit of anger. He disciplined me for something innocent that I had said that perhaps told more about him than it did about me. Normally, he would tell me to go pick out a belt and go to my room whenever I had a whippin' coming. I recommend that approach for parents even today. Those were the longest and hardest moments of my life, waiting for him to come in and administer the corporal punishment. But this spanking was different. He hit me harder. He hit me longer. It was one of the few times my sweet sister cried for me and tried to get him to stop.

I love my father. He is 81 at this writing. He came to me the next day and apologized. He had tears in his eyes, which wasn't often for a Goad. I share this story with you now to remind all of us parents to be gentle with our charges and try never to rob them of their delight and trust in us.

The Gift of Fantasy

Mother usually took care of such domestic duties. But that particular day found my father at home doing some chores. It must have been a Saturday. There I was sitting in his lap, being consoled and told that my tongue would eventually quit hurting and that the bleeding would soon stop. He had helped me wipe my tears away and was attempting to gently ply my mind with a healthy dose of reality. It was a special time for me being able to have that closeness with Dad, but I was a hard study I'm sure. For he was dealing with a son who happened to have a mega-imagination, along with a short attention span. Sob. One more dab at the blood coming from my mouth.

What goes on in a child's brain is a mine field of make-believe and wonder. My mind was no less active. I thought of things that never were, and asked, "Why not?" Sitting next to the radio and listening to "Clyde Beatty, Animal Trainer," I could actually see him with a whip in his hand and shudder at how far he could put his head into a lion's mouth. As the soap operas were broadcast, even as a kid, I knew that "Just Plain Bill" wasn't all that plain. "Amos and Andy" made me laugh and "Fibber McGee and Molly" made me cry. Then, along came a device that robbed us of much of our wonder. It was too graphic. It stole our imagination by taking away the mystery of the mind's ability to fill in all the blanks. Sound effects were replaced with pictures. Fantasy was replaced with reality. Life would never be the same. Television was upon us.

My heroes were usually cowboys. I mean, how could one improve on Lash Larue or Range Rider? Hopalong Cassidy was a favorite of mine as well as Gene and Roy. But for some reason, I found Superman to be the consummate good guy. He was almost supernatural in his abilities. He was sort of like Jesus to me. He wasn't as powerful as Jesus, of course, but he could see through things. Jesus could actually read minds. Superman couldn't do that. And he couldn't even walk on water like my Savior did. He could make us think he was walking on water, but he would actually be flying above it, hovering over it and fooling us.

Superman had already caused me much grief. I still had the scars on my knees from trying to hold back the milkman's truck with my bare hands. It dragged me several feet before I would admit defeat. Oh, the agony of defeat. Chalk it up to youth. I was only seven or eight at the time. Or better still, chalk it up to stupidity. For my young innocence took me to levels of danger and terror that I should not wish upon any poor soul. I must have kept my guardian angel working over-time, if I had one. And it's amazing that I survived the cuts and bruises and contusions and breaks and bumps that were mine to endure. Maybe I am living proof of heavenly guardianship.

I had some energy to burn that Saturday before the ham-burgers were ready. I loved Dad's hamburgers. He cooked the onions right in the skillet with the meat. Yum! He learned how to do that at White Castle as a young man. He even met Mom at White Castle. I love White Castle hamburgers. But Dad's were far better than any White Castle burger I ever ate. Lunch would be ready in fifteen minutes. Time enough to challenge the elements. Plenty of time to push the envelope.

A bath towel served as my cape. A blue shirt that was too tight offered a reasonable facsimile of his suit. It was good luck for me that Dad had been doing some work on the gutter, because the ladder was still leaning against the house. I climbed up the ladder carefully. I was overly afraid of heights. Before I could get to the second rung, Captain Blondie, our cocker spaniel, was nipping at my pants leg. I shook him off and made it to the second rung. Then the third. Then the last. I held on tightly to the ladder. One hand was on the shingles of the roof, one on the ladder. I looked down and thought of aborting the mission.

Make believe isn't all that easy at times. Here I was, with all my gift of imagination intact, and I was trembling at the thought of being that high off the ground. I was ashamed of myself. I mean, Superman could leap tall buildings in a single bound, he was faster than a speeding bullet, and he could stop locomotives with his bare hands. What a wimp I was, what a fraidy cat. I'm glad my buddies weren't there to witness the yellow-bellied exercise in mayhem. I drew from some strength within me to mount the roof and walk to the edge. It seemed so high. I had been sane enough to pile a bunch of throw rugs on the ground to where I would jump. But I still had goose bumps up my spine. Then it happened. For some strange reason, I lost all fear and from a running start I leapt from the roof with a mighty yell (although I didn't recall Superman ever yelling while flying), onto the ground.

Ouch! I hadn't yet taken a class in physics. First of all, I missed the rugs. Second of all, my legs buckled under me and my chin hit my right knee. Third of all, I bit a hole right through my tongue. Fourth of all, the pain was intense. Fifth of all, I started to bleed profusely. Sixth of all, I started to scream a scream that only a loving parent could fully understand. That was when my father arrived on the scene.

Luckily for me, I already had a towel handy. It kept me from bleeding all over my clothes. "What's the matter, Stevie?" my sire asked. "I hurt mythelf," I answered with a lisp. "How did you do that?" he continued. "I, sob, sob, sob, wuth trying to be Thuperman and jumped off the woof and bit my thung." Bleed. Sob. I milked my pain for all it was worth because Dad didn't take too kindly to foolishness. And this was foolishness, clear and simple. But Dad must have sensed that my stupidity needed some attention, so he proceeded to console me and nurse my wounds. I wasn't all the worse for wear. I had skinned one elbow and made hamburger of my tongue. Other than that, there were no broken bones. Of course, the hamburgers that day didn't taste quite the same.

I wish I could end this story of boyhood insanity by saying that I never did another stupid stunt like this in my life, but I cannot tell a lie. That day in Dad's lap did help me to begin to see the difference between fantasy and reality, between the absurd and the serious. A lot of grownups haven't learned that lesson yet. The apostle Paul said something about this matter of learning how to mature gracefully. "When I became a man I put away childishness." When I observe grown folk behaving in such childish ways, I thank my God that I am no longer engaging in adolescent foolishness. All of my foolishness these days is purely grownup stuff, as all can readily see.

His Name Was Jimmy

He was the first to befriend me when our family moved into the neighborhood. We both lived on Bradbury Street. He was almost two years younger than I, and I was only eight. He taught me how to ride a bicycle. He not only had a bicycle before I got mine, but he had been riding it for half his lifetime. He seemed more resilient than I and had a wisdom beyond his years. He became my Jonathan and I became his David. We became closer than had we been blood brothers.

Jimmy never seemed to have any chores to do. He didn't appear to have any rules at all. He was usually at our house. I soon learned that he was an orphan. Well, not really an orphan, sort of a half orphan. His mother had died when he and his twin sister were mere babies. So our family took Jimmy in as one of our own, though he never slept at our house except when invited over to stay the night. His father was rarely at home since he was on the road trying to make a living for his four children. And to our delight, his father was in the candy business. Jimmy and I would often raid his dad's candy truck, with Jimmy always reminding me his father wouldn't care, as long as we didn't take too much candy at one time.

Jimmy was always a little less groomed than some of the rest of the kids on the block. I noticed that at once, but what's a little dirt between friends? It wasn't until I was older that I figured out he was a bit scruffy because he had to wash and iron his own clothes and take his own baths. Had I been the one to determine the frequency of baths, I might have looked far less dapper than poor Jimmy. Mom and Dad had a special place in their hearts for my buddy. He was always included in the Saturday hamburger fries for which Dad was notorious. He loved it at our house. He taught me how to share. Jimmy attended Vacation Bible School and church with us, when we could get his attention focused in that direction.

For some strange reason I always had it in the back of my mind that Jimmy was underprivileged. But what I learned from him was that, in many ways, I was the one who was lacking. He had a heart to share more than I did. He had a mind to work more than I did. He gave a lot more of himself in our friendship than I ever did. And he was there for me when I became a half orphan a few years later in our relationship, to comfort and console.

It's funny how, at the time, you are enjoying some of the finest moments of your life and the finest intimacies in your life and yet you aren't really aware of it. It is only after years go by and memories leap to the front of your consciousness that you recall how blessed you were. And it isn't simply an embellishment of how things were as we nostalgically recall the "good old days." Sometimes we discover that the "good old days" weren't all that great. But I know one thing, it was the friendship of Jimmy VanBusum back in the decade of the '50s that helped make my life full of precious memories. And I feel sad for those who drift through life not having found their Jonathan.

This isn't really a story so much as it is a recollection. I don't mean a "ready recollection" as goes forth the request for the parson during church. It's more like a testimony to friendship. If we don't learn to extend ourselves in friendship to people, even to people who may seem dirtier than we, or less fortunate than we, we will occupy life without joy and face eternity without hope. For it is in the friendship of Jesus that we have our hope, and He must stoop pretty low to make that friendship possible.

Jimmy taught me how to laugh at my foibles and how to cry at my blessings. One day on the grade school grounds Jimmy and his sister, Nancy, had made a little mound of dirt. They had stuck a popsicle stick in the middle of it. I asked them what it was and they told me it was a make believe grave where their mother was. They had tears running down their dusty cheeks. I couldn't have been more than eight or nine at the time, but I recall weeping with them. I didn't know why then, but I know why now. I wanted to share with them, in as close proximity as possible, the thing that was nearest to their hearts. And it made me happy to be able to share my living mother with Jimmy until her home going and his under-standing tears a few years later.

Sometimes I miss my old buddy, Jimmy. I think I'll call him on the phone right now.

My First Kiss

It was a May/September affair as I recall. Her name was
Judy Pigg. (Don't even think about it!) I was seven and she
was four. We met at the church house. What a fine place to
meet girlfriends. I met most of mine there. How we got
thrown together as a couple is far beyond my ability to recall.
Our parents were friends. The disparity in age might have
found me playing with trucks and the boys and Judy playing
with dolls and the girls. But there we were, thrown together
in the strangest little relationship for two or three years.
That's how long our romance lasted. Now that I think about
it, it lasted longer than many marriages do today. And it's a
warm memory.

One Sunday she would be at my house after the morning
assembly, the next I'd be at hers. We enjoyed games and pets
and eating together. For some reason our parents thought the
affair more than proper and allowed us this innocent youthful
romance. For the life of me I don't know how kids that young
can have any feelings of love in the sense that adults can love.
And I am not even suggesting that we had that sort of thing
going on. But when church time rolled around, Judy stuck to
me like my shadow. And I reveled in the attention. Wherever I
was, Judy could be found close at hand. And I didn't seem to
resent the smothering even when the boys were around.

We had been enjoying each others' company for about
three months when it happened. She had already asked her
mother for permission. One day after swinging for hours on
our swing set, we decided to go inside and get something to
drink. She took my hand and stood on her tiptoes and kissed
me. Right on the lips. Now I wasn't one that relished kissing
on the lips. I didn't even like for grandma to kiss me on the
lips. It was too familiar. It was too wet. But for some crazy
reason, I didn't mind Judy doing the job. She said nothing. I
said nothing. We went inside and behaved as if nothing were
any different. And I suppose, nothing was really any different
between us. But what made it stand out in my mind was that

it was the first kiss any girl had ever given me as an expression of friendship, or puppy love or whatever it was. That little kiss, with no prurient sensuality attached to it at all, reminds me of how important it is for Christians and friends to be affectionate, to exchange holy kisses.

Yes, I know. Handshakes are supposed to replace kisses today, right? And it's sad. It's sad that disease and dirty old men have caused the church to casually set aside a direct command. We are embarrassed by it. We are uncomfortable with it. Grown men can kiss each other in Russia, but if a kiss of greeting is exchanged in the church foyer, eyebrows raise and nervous coughs are offered. It's sad to live in a society that has made almost every beautiful thing the Lord has created something to be viewed as dirty or vulgar.

Judy and I lost track of each other over the years. I hope she is well. And I hope she remembers as fondly as I do the tenderness of that innocent first love. Ever since then kisses have had a great significance to me. A kiss is a beautiful thing. Judas made a mockery of the kiss when he betrayed our Savior. But it was the Savior who taught the disciples how to love each other in the most unselfish manner possible. And this kind of affection was demonstrable in so many ways, one of which was the kiss of greeting.

Maybe I should offer a disclaimer at the end of this little trek backward in time. It wasn't really my first kiss. My mother told me that I had many, many, many kisses delivered to my personhood on the very first day of my life. So, what I mean by "first kiss," is that kiss that allowed me to know that God had something special awaiting me and that life is worth experiencing.

Maybe kisses don't make the world go around, but like love, they sure do make the ride worthwhile. Thanks, Mother. And, thanks again, Judy, wherever you are.

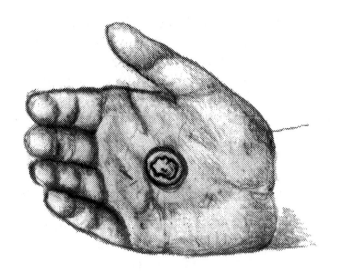

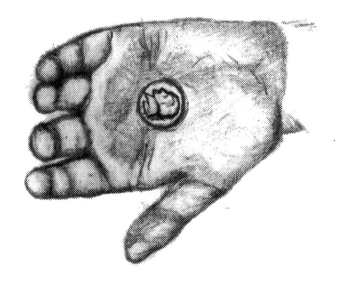

The Day I Killed Jesus

It was one of the saddest days of my life. I had no intention of committing such a dastardly deed. It never dawned on my ten-year-old mind that I could be guilty of participating in such a mortal sin. But I'm ahead of myself already. Let me start at the beginning.

My parents took their faith very seriously, and I am grateful for that. It was their faith and discipline that kept the devil out of the house called Steven Clark Goad. I was an empty vessel ready to be filled with whatever came along and needed a place to stay. Perhaps all children are like that. But my parents did their dead level best not to let little Stevie grow up a sinner in a world of sin, not if they could help it.

I was rapidly approaching that magic "age of accountability" and should have known better. But when my best church buddies, David McDonald and Lane Morgan were around, the three of us could get into all kinds of mischief. It was hard for us to keep our minds on spiritual things, and our parents seemed to have a sixth sense that could tell what we were planning even before we carried it out. Like the time my mother caught me keeping the dollar bill she had given me for the collection plate. I pretended to put it in the plate. How could she see from across the auditorium that I hadn't actually given my offering? But that's another story.

After services on Sunday evenings one of the ladies would take the Lord's Supper emblems that were left and put them on a table in the basement of the old Fountain Square church house in Indianapolis where we were attending. One of us boys, I'm sure it wasn't me, suggested we "play church." To make church seem even more real, we were going to play Lord's Supper. That idea found all three of us in the little room where the table was, with the fruit of the vine and Matzo crackers. As somberly as we could, we prayed and thanked God for the bread. Then we ate it. We ate it all. Not just a pinch. All of it! Then we prayed again and hurriedly gulped down the remaining grape juice in the little cups. Oops! I spilled some on my coat. I tried to wipe it out as best I could. The coat was dark so I thought my parents wouldn't notice. Wrong!

My friends had to leave with their families. Since the Goads were gregarious, we usually stayed until the last person went home, so I found myself standing in the light of the vestibule when dad saw it. "What's on your coat, Stevie?" My face burned with an instant blush. "Nothing," I answered sheepisly. "Steven!" When my dad or mom called me "Steven" I knew I was in big trouble. "Steven, I'll ask you just one more time. What is on your coat?" By this time he had touched the spot which was still wet, and even smelled it to determine what it was I spilled. "It's grape juice, Dad."

What ensued after that I would not wish on my bitterest enemy. My father solicited the help of brother Adams, one of the church elders. After I confessed the entire episode while weeping copiously in hopes of garnering some sympathy, my father and brother Adams and I went into a little room. Brother Adams looked sternly into my fearful blue eyes. "Steven, do you know what you have done?" Then he read the entire Lord's Supper text from 1 Corinthians 11, ending with: "Whoever eats the bread or drinks the cup of the Lord in an unworthy manner will be guilty of sinning against the body and blood of the Lord" (verse 27). This was read from the King James Version with as much sobriety as an elder could muster at such a serious occasion.

In the moments that followed, I was told that I was just as guilty as those who had nailed my Savior to the cross. I was told that in making a mockery of the body and blood of Jesus that I was like those who literally murdered our Lord. I shuddered in abject terror. Now I wasn't able to challenge the theology that was being presented on that dark and wintery Sunday evening. Maybe the elder and my dad were taking liberties with the text. But I was in no position to challenge their exegesis. I hadn't yet learned what exegesis was. So I just cried. And cried. And felt the wrath of God more severely than perhaps ever before or again in my life.

As I reflect from my vantage point of over half a century old, I might suppose that what the elder and my dad did to me that evening was child abuse. I might make a case for overkill. But I won't. And I can't. What I learned that evening helped me come to grips with my own spirituality. It helped me to see that life is not simply a matter of fun and games, but involves the realities of life and death. And my Savior died for me. And I was impressed with the truth that His death was *the most important* event in human history. It was a watershed moment in my life.

One other thing I learned that evening with Dad and brother Adams. I learned not to be guilty of the body and blood of Jesus by disobeying him or making some childish game out of the Lord's Supper. Maybe it was bad theology being presented that evening, but I never want to slay my Savior again.

Tent Meetings

I am much too young to remember the old brush arbor meetings of yesteryear. It seems to me that they were the social gatherings of the age. To have a traveling evangelist ride into town and set up shop for weeks, or even months, was the event of all events. Of course, this was before the family altar was invented, namely, television. People took time to read, if they had any time left over from their labors. They also took time to be holy, on purpose. Brush arbor meetings were occasions for believers and non-believers alike to relish in the old time gospel and hear the magnificent stories of Old Testament heroes. The churches in America spread like wildfire during that period of our history.

At the ripe old age of 53, I can recall not having television in my house. Not that it wasn't already invented. I believe Steven Clark Goad and TV were invented about the same time, or at least their availability to the public coincided. Thus, reading and radio played a greater role in the family than they do now. The Goads used their imaginations in order to come up with things to do that were entertaining and educational. Museums were fun to visit. We often went to the airport and just watched the planes take off and land. Parks were special as well as arboretums and botanical gardens. Garfield Park was one of our favorites.

One other thing the Goads did for entertainment and spiritual growth was to attend tent meetings. These were revival meetings that often were conducted as a church was attempting to get established in a specific locale. For some reason, the white congregations of my youth didn't seem to find this kind of beginning very attractive, for most of the tent meetings we visited were held by black churches. We found that if we wanted to get our soul batteries recharged, all we had to do was find a tent meeting in town somewhere. Some of the fieriest oratory based on Scripture I ever heard was offered at such gatherings. I had the privilege of hearing an old, soft-spoken little black man by the name of Marshall

Keeble. What a gentle soul he was, but his messages were powerful. And I remember hearing a young firebrand by the name of G.P. Holt who would preach so forcefully and boldly that his clothes were literally soaking wet when he finished speaking.

My sister and I didn't know it at the time, but there was one significant thing we learned besides the Bible at those tent meetings. We learned tolerance and acceptance. We learned that persons with black or brown or tan skin could be just as wonderful as us white folk. I never understood why kids would hang their heads out of the school bus when we were riding through a Black community and yell insulting remarks. My sister and I had learned that black folks and white folks loved the same God and had the same Savior. We understood that those dear ones with a built-in suntan were precious to have as friends. It is amazing to me that some people will hate others because their skin is darker and yet will pay good money to go to a tanning salon or the beach in order to get as dark as they possibly can, even risking skin cancer.

"Red and yellow, black and white, they are precious in his sight!" I always enjoyed the parable of the net where all kinds of fish were caught. I never fished with a net. I always used a pole. When fishing with a pole, one, if he is lucky, catches but a single fish at a time. It might be a bluegill or a bass or a trout. But he never catches all three from the same cast. When fishing with a net, the net becomes nondiscriminatory. Nets have no prejudice. That's why many ocean fishermen are getting into trouble as they catch and kill dolphins right along with the tuna they are after. Jesus told His disciples that He would make them fishers of men. So, as we disciples go out into our world today, we need to take a fishing net with us. And no matter what the shape or color or size may be, we must be eager to catch and bring "home" whatever fish might present themselves.

My parents could have been biased toward other races. They were reared in the South, but, for some reason, they seemed to have no animosity for another human being based on color or race or other such unimportant factors. They assessed the value of others based on their character and integrity, for what they chose to do, not for how they looked. And it was Marshall Keeble who reminded us that we weren't to judge, as the good Lord advised, but we were to be cautious fruit inspectors. As we inspected the fruit of individuals, we would accept them or avoid them based on their inner values, their decisions, their behavior. Color had nothing to do with it. So, I was fortunate not to have had to wrestle with the heavy issue of racial prejudice in my youth. We had black preachers in our home on various occasions, regardless of what our white neighbors might have thought about it. In retrospect, I suppose my group of close friends resembled a kind of "rainbow coalition." Color was simply a nonissue with me. While on a trip together, a black friend and I tried to stay in a motel and were refused. It hadn't dawned on me that people were refused housing simply because they were the "wrong" color. My friend gave me a history, prompted by that rejection in my presence, of his life as a black young man and how he had been treated so shabbily over the years. His family couldn't even go on a vacation without giving serious thought as to where they could stay. I was shocked and flabbergasted at how inhumanely his race had been treated over the years by even those who called themselves Christians.

Oh, yes, I was telling you about tent meetings. They worked. Souls were saved. Races found that they truly were one in Christ Jesus. A tent meeting was better than any TV program I have ever seen. And I learned tolerance and love at an early age by going to those tent meetings with my family. What a marvelous memory it is. Have we grown too comfortable and too at ease in Zion in our fine church facilities to conduct tent meetings anymore? Maybe they have become a relic of the past, like brush arbor meetings, but I sure do miss them. Thanks, brother Keeble. Thanks, G.P. And thanks a lot, Mom and Dad.

A Close Encounter

We were "vacationing" at Dale Hollow Lake, close to Kettle, Kentucky. It was a dream vacation for an eight-year-old boy. My grandfather, George Washington Coop, Jr., owned some fishing cabins by the lake. The cabins didn't actually fish, but they were there to house the fishermen who came to the lake for sport. My dad was there for sort of a working vacation. He was building a brick outdoor grill for grandpa and was helping to spruce up the place. This was the vacation when a lizard ran up Dad's leg. Since there were scorpions under just about every brick we picked up, Dad took the lizard episode quite seriously and completely bypassed his normal modesty that day. But that's another story entirely.

Some friends of Dad's were going to Wolf Lake to do some serious fishing. They asked if I could tag along. Dad was probably happy for the relief from one inquisitive son and allowed me to go. I took a cane fishing pole. They had all the fancy fly casting equipment money could buy. We fished a long time that day. It was quite a time for me for, after several hours of fishing, I held the bragging rights to the day's catch. It required all three of them to catch one scrawny bluegill. They even threw it back. With my borrowed cane pole I caught three sizable fish. They had all the lures and flies I had ever seen. I had some bread and a few almost too dry worms as my bait. They were not happy campers. But I was enjoying quite a high as a result of my newfound fishing skills.

We had arrived back at shore and the adults I had been with went to the little general store to get some refreshments and chew the fat with the proprietor. I had a few minutes to play in the water. I was a city slicker and rarely had access to bodies of water, even a swimming pool. So I had not yet learned to swim. Since the water was shallow at the docking area, I felt secure as I waded and enjoyed the coolness of being wet on that muggy summer day. I had only ventured out a few feet, it seemed to me, into waist high water, when I suddenly sank like a lead weight. I had stepped off an underwater plateau. It must have been a drop of fifteen feet.

What went through my mind at the time is almost spiritual in nature. I didn't have much of a vocabulary, but I recall the feeling of being frightened of drowning along with the sense that my life was rushing before me. I entertained thoughts of how precious my parents were to me and how I wished I could tell my sister how much I loved her, in spite of the humiliation I could cause her on any given day. It was as if a narration of my life's events was being unfolded in visual displays of my most memorable encounters.

All the while, I was scrambling to grab hold of something to pull myself up out of the water. As I was clawing the edge of the slope trying to get a grip, I remembered the time I hit a grand slam home run in softball at school. It was hard pretending not to be proud of myself that day, hard not to act as though grand slams were a part of my everyday life. Yet, I had never hit another before, nor since. I remember the time Grandma Goad killed two hens for supper. In Grandma's day a convenience food was a chicken one didn't have to personally catch, behead, scald, pluck and then prepare for frying.

I remembered how much fun it was to sit with Dad in Bee Wyatt's general store in Kettle and eat crackers and cheese while the men talked of world events. And how neat it was to have had a bottle of near beer and get my very first knife. I thought of my girlfriend at school. I thought about how I would never be able to see my teachers again. And I thought about God and that I had never been baptized. I even wondered if God would allow this drowning to be my baptism if I truly had faith. I mean, could a young boy baptize himself?

Don't tell me how a kid can think of all of these things while he is drowning. But I did it. I thought of Ronnie Kelp and Jimmy VanBusum and how I would not be able to play with them in the neighborhood any more. While my mind was doing a rerun of my short life, I was, all the while, climbing the side of this steep underwater wall of earth. Apparently I was making progress, but at the time I didn't know how deeply I had sunk. I don't know why I didn't just give up. I thought of that, too.

God is good. God created at least one mind, my mind, to be able to contemplate how much I was enjoying living so that I could refrain from totally panicking and simply thrashing about in the water expending all my energy while thinking of nothing. It must have been that my guardian angel wasn't on his vacation while I was on mine, for somehow, the thoughts of my life enabled me to climb the underwater embankment without being overwhelmed and overcome by fear and panic. As I recall, I thought I was going to die. At least I was making the best of it by remembering.

My lungs were bursting when I reached the surface of the water. I had actually taken in water because I remember spitting and coughing. Apparently I had been underwater for some time because the adults I had been with were standing there in the water, having waded out to the drop-off. Someone had told them he saw a boy go under. One man was just about ready to dive into the deep to look for me.

It was only after I gulped a few lungs full of air that I really comprehended what had almost transpired. I tried hard not to, but I cried. I hid my head in a fisherman's chest and cried for the longest time. I was embarrassed and ashamed. I was embarrassed that I was crying. I was ashamed that I was unable to swim. Somehow, not being able to swim was a sign of a lack of sophistication that a fellow of my age should have already achieved.

My mother had always taught me to say my bedtime prayers. I felt terrible whenever I fell asleep without having remembered to say my prayers. At first they were "now I lay me down to sleep" prayers. But I had matured far beyond my years and hadn't said that kind of prayer for weeks, perhaps months. That evening, I said my longest and most heartfelt prayer. I thanked God that He had spared my life. I thanked Him for Mom and Dad and Jackie and my dog Topsy and for school and food and shelter and clothing . . . but most of all, I thanked Him for life.

I don't understand how people can get so desperate that they want to commit suicide. I have had to officiate at the funerals of suicide victims. It is a difficult task. Life is so precious. The gift of living and being is so marvelous, yet we sometimes take it for granted. Some of us have to have close encounters with death before we are able to grasp the significance of this probation time on the planet.

The closest I came to drowning since Wolf Lake was when I was almost overwhelmed in a sea of blessings from God. On the worst day, life is better than the alternative. Don't wait until you are at the edge of death to be grateful to God for life. And don't forget in your next prayer to thank Him for its blessings. And be sure to thank Him for the little things.

Remember.

Rusty Nails

Jesus and I have something in common. We both wear the scars of having been nailed. His scars came from obeying His Father, mine from disobedience. But I'm getting ahead of myself already.

Flash back with me to Beech Grove, Indiana. Some of my friends from school had asked me to meet them at our secret place under the bridge on Hobart Street. Bean Creek ran under the bridge. It was there we caught crawdads and avoided leeches and made blood-brother oaths to be friends forever. When I got home from school, I found a note from Mother telling me to clean my room and do my school homework and not to leave the premises. So I sadly began to comply and started raking under my bed. I was eleven.

It was then the phone rang. My buddies had decided to go over to Tommy McFarland's house instead of meeting at the bridge. They said to hurry over and see what they had found. The invitation caused me to lose all memory of what Mom had written. So I scurried off to play. When I got to Tommy's house, I found the guys jumping off the top of a shed. At least I thought it was a shed. It actually was an old outhouse.

When I arrived on the scene, the fellas seemed to be having a terrific time. I was always afraid of heights. Maybe that's why God made me only five feet seven inches short. I still don't like short jokes all that much. Anyway, the guys started to tease me and dare me to climb on top and make a jump. Since there were no pillows and no water and no straw to jump into, I wasn't all that eager to meet the challenge. So they began to goad me. They called me chicken. They made clucking sounds. They pretended to flap their wings. I resisted. Now, remember, these were my best friends. Then they Double-Dog-Dared me to jump.

So, on top of the shed (outhouse) I climbed. Kids are stupid. Kids who grew up in my neighborhood seemed especially stupid. There were nails all over the place. Rusty, nasty, dirty, lockjaw inviting nails. I stood at the edge of the structure's roof. I teetered. I changed my mind a few times and tried to abort the jump. But eventually I jumped, to the glee of my pals and to my chagrin. I landed right foot on a rusty nail. It not only went into my tender foot, it went all the way through and stuck out the top. I screamed bloody murder. My play-mates looked as if they'd been part of a Brink's robbery. All of them ran away except Tommy. He helped me extricate myself from the impalement. His mother, fortunately, was a nurse and washed the wound out with some chemical. I scurried home as fast as I could.

Do you know what went through my mind the minute I felt the nail enter my foot? Yep! Mother. I remembered imme-diately that I wasn't even supposed to be out of the yard. How desperately I wished I could have obeyed her and not experi-enced this episode in my life. I had limped home as fast as one and a half feet could carry me.

When Mom and Dad got home, I acted as if nothing were wrong. I tried not to limp, but I couldn't help myself. Soon after dinner, Mother asked, "Stevie, what's wrong with your foot?" Never try to lie to your parents when they know some-thing is wrong. It just won't work. After a few attempts at denial, I finally 'fessed up and told her the sordid tale. I knew that she would feel so sorry for her injured little boy and that I could avoid the inevitable. Au contraire! I was hurting in two places that evening before I went to bed.

Nails remind me of disobedience. It was our rebellion that caused Jesus to die at Calvary. Nails also remind me of obedi-ence. Jesus obeyed His Father in all that He suffered. And you'd think a Hoosier lad would have learned his lesson. It was but a few months later that an invitation from Ricky Klugish found me at his house with a nail in my knee when I should have been at home. I got the spanking of a lifetime for that one, with no sympathy from even my usually soft-hearted mom. Nails also remind me of punishment.

God is good. He could have allowed a rebellious son such as I to die at an early age of tetanus, but by His kind and beneficent mercy, He allowed me another chance. And another, and another. The scars remind me.

Chapter Three

Cerebral Journeys

Choices

This is a story about choices. While serving as a volunteer chaplain at one of our state prisons, the warden said something to me that has always stuck in my mind. Perhaps I had heard it expressed in other words, but the prison setting made it especially meaningful. He said, "One of the differences between the men in this prison and us is that when they came to those forks in the road, they took the wrong path." I don't know if that is exactly how he worded it; I mean, I suppose he should have said, "They took the wrong tine." But you get the gist of the meaning. And it has to do with choices. At those Y's or forks, people of little principle and gumption often take the road most traveled. It's the path of least resistance. It's what makes rivers and people crooked.

I've come to some of those splits in the road myself, as
have all of us. Some involved moral choices, and others were
just involving the directions my life would take. I thank God
my parents gave me a moral compass, or "there but for the
grace of God. . . ." Without that moral direction and a conscience shaped by Christian principle, I might have been dead
long ago, maybe physically or maybe spiritually.

During high school I made several choices that altered
the direction of my life. Before I entered high school, a new
system of study had been developed. The school was offering
three different diplomas. One was an academic diploma. The
others, in descending order, were the vocational and the general diplomas. Being the intellectual genius that I humbly
envisioned myself to be, I chose the academic diploma, of
course. However, this choice limited the elective subjects I
could take. This diploma more or less left out woodworking
shop and auto mechanics. I couldn't get credit for printing
shop or other such vocational type learning opportunities,
which I have often regretted. Instead of taking general science,
I had to take biology and chemistry. Instead of general math, I
had to take algebra, trig and calculus. Dumb move on my
part. But, with the help of my guardian angel I suppose, I was
still able to graduate with honors.

Anyway, this isn't about that decision. It is about a
choice I made which, on reflection, I suppose was the wisest I
could have made at the time. I was deciding whether to be a
jock or a tenor.

I grew up in Indiana where, if religion isn't the opiate of
the people, then basketball is. I dreamed and ate and slept
basketball. Dad put up a goal on our back patio. I made it to
all the high school games. My sister was in high school three
years before I was. But I lived the high school experience
through her and loved to watch high school basketball.

By the time I had entered my freshman year, I was still
only five feet seven inches short. I had been that height for
about two years. For some reason, my growth genes must
have been on permanent leave of absence. There were a few
kids, guys who were extra talented, who made the basketball

team at only five five or maybe five six or seven, but they were rare. I did have a few things going for me, however. First, my father had become friends with the coach. I thought that surely couldn't hurt. Also, I could run about as fast as anyone else. My jump shot was pretty well down pat, and I had once shot 27 baskets in a row from the free throw line without missing. So, I thought I had a pretty good shot, if you'll pardon the expression, at the freshman team.

Basketball in Indiana is known as "Hoosier Hysteria." I mean, Indiana is the land of a yearly crowned "Mr. Basketball." The best high school player in the state was awarded that title by the sports writers. Oscar Robertson had been a Mr. Basketball. Jimmy Rahl had been a Mr. Basketball. During my tenure at Manual High School, we had two Mr. Basketballs, at the same time. They were twins. Tom and Dick Van-Arsdale were crowned Mr. Basketball in their senior (my junior) year. They were six feet five inches tall and made me look like a midget. So, I avoided standing close to them. They went on to fame at Indiana University and later with the New York Knicks and the Phoenix Suns. Being in school with them was like being around celebrities.

But back to my sad story. During the first few weeks of my freshman year I was at tryouts for the basketball team. The large city school of about 1,500 students had freshman, reserve and varsity teams. The Vans were so good they got to play some varsity their first year. My object was to just get on the freshman team, even if I weren't a first stringer. I made the first cut. Then I made the second cut. There was only one more cut to go, and since I was faster than all but one guy, and could shoot as good as their best shooter, I thought I was a shoo-in.

Enter Mr. Mertz. Mr. Wendell Mertz, who later became a mentor and friend, was the director of the school choir. As a kid who loved to sing, I was already in boy's chorus. It was an inferior group for guys who simply wanted to sing, whether they could or not. Choir was a very selective group of singers. It was even called concert choir. I had hopes of making the choir by maybe my junior year. But Mr. Mertz, who also

directed the boys chorus, discovered that little Stevie Goad
had been trained well by his mother at church. I could sing
tenor. And Mr. Mertz needed two more tenors for choir. Guess
what? That's right. "Steve," he said to me one day after chorus, "I'd like you and J Wincklebach to be part of the tenor
section in choir." Wow! I was thrilled. It was an opportunity of
a lifetime. And he had addressed me as "Steve" instead of
"Stevie." I mean, I was coming of age for sure. Before checking
with my agent, I accepted his offer. It meant shuffling a few
classes. That alone got me a little behind in Algebra. And it
also meant something else I hadn't counted on: conflict with
my dreams of a career in basketball.

Amazingly, I made the final cut for the freshman basketball team. I was already dreaming of someday being the star
on the varsity team and making that winning shot at the state
finals. I just knew my growth spurt would kick in like it did for
Vasco DeWalton. Vasco had been a cheerleader for his first
two years in high school. He was shorter than I was then.
Then, all of a sudden, he must have grown eight or ten inches
in one year. He became one of the star players on the varsity
his senior year. I recall him making 25 points in one game.
That was a big deal, back then. Hey, I already had a leg up on
Vasco. I had thought of becoming a cheerleader. But my algebra teacher made fun of boys who were "yell leaders" as he
called them. He said only sissies did that sort of thing. His
teasing worked well, for I abandoned that prospect entirely,
though with my tumbling skills I was told I could have made
the squad handily.

Back to my other troubles. Within a week of being in
choir, the annual musical was being planned. Mr. Mertz
would allow anyone who was interested in a lead part to try
out. Being the gregarious kid that I was, and stagestruck to
boot, I tried out for a solo part. Yep! Good things happen to
the Goad kid. I was given the lead role my first year in school.
My head swelled 'til it almost popped. "Thank you so much,
Mr. Mertz." I was to play Harold Post, a shy suitor to a girl
whose father wasn't very interested in the likes of my character. The musical was titled "Up In the Air." The reason for the

title was that I had to do a parachute jump to prove my bravery to the girl's father. Silly, isn't it? And here is where my young life got more complicated.

Musical practice conflicted somewhat with basketball practice. I often was late for basketball. When we were doing the stage setup, we frequently ran overtime. So every other day I was making excuses to the coach for being late. "I'm sorry, Coach, but you know I have the lead in the choir musical. Mr. Mertz won't let me go until practice is over. He says it wouldn't be fair to show favoritism and let the lead, of all people, leave early." My coach was not impressed. "Steve, I'm glad you have the lead in the choir musical, but I need you here for basketball practice. It wouldn't be fair to show favoritism with my team, either. From now on I want you to be at practice on time."

My, oh, my! I was on the horns of a youthful dilemma. I hadn't thought my high school career would take off so suddenly. I thought I would have to work and claw my way to stardom and acceptance. Now, here I was, having to choose between a singing career or basketball fame. Whatever would I do? I actually prayed about it. Then I asked Mr. Mertz to please let me go to basketball practice on time. He wouldn't budge. He dug in even deeper and said, "Steve, if you want to be in choir, it will always be in conflict with sports, especially basketball. I may want to use you every year for a lead part in the musical. You will be having this conflict all the time." My "buts" didn't count for anything. "If you choose basketball, I will understand. You can remain in choir, but I will have to give the leading role to someone else."

Life is tough for 14-year-old superstars. I actually shed tears over the decision I had to make. I had envisioned myself being a member of the lettermen's club. I wanted so badly to become a sweaty jock, just like the star basketball players I had idolized. I thought about Tom and Dick VanArsdale. We had one of the tallest high school teams in the state. Our center was six feet eight inches; unheard of in those days. We had the potential to go to the state championship (and did in the Vans' senior year of 1961). I thought about my chances of advancing to varsity team, even if I grew a few inches. It was too high a risk. I would have loved to have been able to say that I had played high school basketball with the VanArsdale twins and then went on to Indiana University with them on full athletic scholarship, but it was only a school boy's dream, soon to be gone forever. On a chilly September afternoon, after my choir practice, I slumped into the gym and headed toward Coach Bill Bennett. He was a tenderhearted man. But he also wanted to win basketball games. "Coach Bennett. I've made my decision. I'll have to quit the team and stay with choir." He consoled me and patted me on the back and said, "Steve, I don't think you will regret this decision."

Over the years, I have wondered how things might have turned out differently for me had I chosen that other path. There was a kid at Southport High School by the name of Danny Warner who was a star player on their varsity. They even beat our school a few times. He was only five feet four inches short. I mean, we were both taller than Napoleon had been, and even old Bonaparte didn't get to play on his high school basketball team, if I recall my history correctly. Alas, it was not to be.

I went on to enjoy four years in choir. Wincklebach, it's a funny name, isn't it, and I got four bars on our senior lyre. It wasn't a letter, but I considered it equivalent to one. We were among the few and the proud who got to be in choir four full years, except for those first two weeks, of course. Music was important to me then. It still is. I learned to play the piano. I learned to pick and grin on the guitar. I still love to sing tenor, but bass is rapidly approaching. I majored in music at college. The Vans would always smile and acknowledge knowing me when I would see them on campus at IU. I used to wonder if their ears popped when they stood.

Guess what? I'm still five feet seven inches (some say that's a stretch). But what a blessing life has been. I never got the fame of Michael Jordan or Charles Barkley, but I got to sing in some operas, even a world premiere. I got to learn how to sing in Italian. That and 89 cents will get you a cup of coffee, I know. I avoided all the terrible injuries that jocks had to endure during their careers. And I even got to run cross country and track in high school. They never conflicted with choir. One year I even wrestled. I don't recommend it, unless you want cauliflower ears and enjoy the close-up and personal odors of sweaty bodies.

I've made a lot of choices since my freshman year of high school. Some have been mistakes. Others have brought countless blessings. None have landed me in prison. Oh, for the glory days. Oh, for the good old days. I often visit the past. . . . .in my mind. But I don't dwell there. I have learned not to live in the past. The future holds a vast storehouse of blessings for God's children. But first, we must pray about the decisions we will be making.

Then we can stand aside and watch in awesome wonder as God makes life enjoyable in spite of the things we might suppose we are missing. I had prayed that I might stay on the basketball team. So, once again, I thank my Lord for "unanswered prayers."

That was the end of this story. This is a disclaimer. I used the term "unanswered" prayer with poetic license. For, actually, I do not believe God refuses to answer the prayers of those who are His children. Of those who are walking in the light, I believe that God answers every single prayer. He just doesn't always answer it the way we might hope. He sometimes says, 'No!" And at other times He may say "Yes" or "Maybe" or "Later." But even when God says "No," He has answered our prayer, hasn't He? Yes!

My First Sweetheart

This is a story about my first true love. Of course, I had enjoyed lots of occasions during my childhood days when I held puppy love for various souls of the female persuasion. As a kid I didn't care how old they were. I always enjoyed the attention of "older" women. One gal in particular was the checker at the Kroger's grocery store on Prospect Street in Indianapolis. She always had an eye for me and I knew it. So I occasionally gave her a little of my charm by winking at her and allowing her to rub the top of my burr head. But that was different.

By "first sweetheart," I mean the one who captured my heart and soul as a mature teen who had to shave once a week, whether I wanted to or not. She came to my attention my freshman year in high school. I had never been taken by anyone quite like I was with Nancy Jordan. She was the choir pianist and I was one of two freshmen allowed in choir my first year in high school. Needless to say, choir became my favorite class. Yes, she too, was an older woman. But I didn't allow that her being a sophomore was all that challenging an obstacle. So I gave chase.

It would be boring to detail the frustrations of two years of asking and hoping and watching and waiting. But, the fact of the matter was that Nancy didn't seem to realize I was on the planet. I did everything, but make a fool of myself, to get her attention, to no avail. So, in the summer before my junior year, I gave up the chase. Lots of girls wanted to date me. And I dated lots of girls. But it was unfair to them because I didn't accept their affections out of remorse over not having obtained Nancy's.

It's a funny thing how God lets things develop. And I can vouch to you that it is when we quit trying so hard to get what we want that we sometimes end up being blessed beyond our wildest expectations. It's like catching a butterfly. If you wish to catch a butterfly, I've been told, don't slap at it wildly with a net, just stand still and allow it to light on your shoulder. That's what I did with Nancy, though I didn't know it at the time.

My first week as a Junior found me performing for what we called a school "auditorium." I had to sing a song from some Broadway play. I asked Nancy to be my accompanist. By this time I already had a steady girlfriend who seemed delighted with the little attention I was giving her. Maybe that is what caught Nancy's eye. To this day I don't know what I was doing any differently than before (besides not pursuing her so hungrily), but all of a sudden I realized that Nancy Jordan had discovered Steven Goad.

First loves are special for many reasons, one of which is the sharing of some of the greatest and most powerful emotions given to us by God. My infatuation with Nancy soon turned to a deeper emotion. I don't know to this day if it was love or not, but it doesn't really make any difference. All the joy and emotion was there as though it were. Pizza dates and concerts in the park and school plays and homework bonded us.

In the middle of my third month of romantic euphoria, my blessed mother died. Floyd Cramer's "Last Date" was number one on the charts at the time. How appropriate for Dad and Mom. Hearing it still makes Dad and me cry. Nancy was there to hold my hand and offer comfort at a level no one else could provide. Perhaps that is why I had such a struggle getting over Nancy when we broke up. Her tears, mingled with mine at the funeral home and the grave site, allowed us to move into a more serious relationship. In spite of our youth, we even talked of some day marrying.

Within our relationship was a deep spiritual dimension. Instead of buying her perfume or jewelry on special occasions, I gave her a Bible and concordance and Bible dictionary. We studied together and prayed during our dates. She attended worship assemblies with my family and was baptized. Everything seemed to fall right in place for a long life together. But things change.

Nancy went off to college after her senior year. It wasn't far away. We dated a few weeks into her first year of college before I started noticing something different about her. She became distant. I tried to figure it out and didn't want to admit what I suspected. Soon I discovered that she had found some delightful "college Joe" who had swept her off her feet. He was even more spiritual than I, she informed me. He was older and wiser. Huh! Big deal! So he was a college sophomore. Give me time and I would become a college sophomore, too.

Broken hearts are very hard to mend. I went into denial immediately and for several months, even years, attempted to re-establish a relationship with this dark-eyed brunette who had actually held my heart captive for four years. If I were embarrassingly truthful, she held my heart for many more years than I would like to confess, so I won't. Be that as it may, we drifted apart and eventually married others and moved in different directions.

Fast forward to the early '90s. A death of a mate and a divorce found us both single again. Oddly, we found ourselves visiting our respective families during the same week in our old home town of Indianapolis. The reunion opportunity I had imagined and secretly hoped for in my mind for years finally became a reality one wintery evening in December. We ended up seeing each other again. Before our "date," I deliberately suppressed the thought that kept leaping to my mind, namely, would there still be any of that old chemistry between us. She was a church secretary. I was a parson. It looked like a perfect match on paper. We had similar memories of our youth, and we also had an interest in not being alone for the rest of our lives.

Our meeting, and subsequent unspoken decision about each other, was cathartic. For decades, always in the back of my mind, there was the gnawing question of whether or not Nancy and I could have made it as a team. The passion of loving someone and being in such close proximity does tend to blind. And I'm sure I had two blind sides regarding Nancy when I was courting her. Some of the arrangements we want to force upon others, if we had the power, simply do not unfold as we wish them to. I realized immediately at our reunion that Nancy and I had gone in such opposite directions, and that our philosophical approach to life was so diametrically opposed, that our dinner date ended up as almost an old lover's quarrel. We argued about theology and we argued about why the past wasn't important to her but was to me.

Another matter, that is delicate to bring up without hurt feelings, is that there was no attraction between us. None! I mean there wasn't for me, and I'm sure I am speaking for her as well. I didn't sense any breathlessness on her part or rapid heartbeat. So there we were, sitting in my car in front of her folks' home just like we had been hundreds of times before, only a quarter of a century earlier. She still had the same dark eyes. Her hair had turned salt and pepper from the dark brown it once was. My hair had turned loose. There may have been a few more pounds on her small frame; I know there were many more on mine. It was no longer "pinch an inch" for me, but "grab a slab."

It was the end to a long episode in my life. The chapter was closed on whether or not it "might have been." Most people probably don't get the opportunity to resolve old, lost loves. I thank God I was able to put my latent desire for sweet Nancy Jordan to rest. And I thank God for the tenderness and kindness I learned from her during those innocent high school days. Life goes on. Death, miles, careers, families separate. But love still abounds.

Boy, I'm having a hard time finishing this tale. But here goes another attempt. Garth Brooks sings, "I thank God for unanswered prayers." I don't know if that thought has a place in this story or not, but I do know God knows what is best for us, and in His providence He allows things to happen, even things that hurt us deeply, to take us to where we need to be. And I must add, these things *hurt* us, but they never really *harm* us. My life is so full now that I suppose I thank God, for Nancy and for myself, that He didn't answer my prayers that she be mine for a lifetime.

Also, God was able to use me to guide Nancy to a clearer understanding of His presence in the world. She had admitted to me that God was not a vital part of her life, other than attending some denominational church services with her family. This alone, my influence on her to see Jesus and to have Him as Savior, was worth the relationship and the ensuing pain of wondering what if. And I don't think Nancy has ever turned her back on God since.

Love is a complicated emotion. Some even suggest that love isn't an emotion at all, that it consists more of doing and giving than some sort of syrupy feeling. Regardless of our philosophical outlook concerning this dimension of our lives, love is a compelling force in the life of any person of spiritual awareness. And I thank my God that Nancy helped me learn how to love more openly and unselfishly. And I thank Him that He used her to guide me through one of the most painful times in my life, the loss of Mom. God is good. God is love.

Gutenberg, Luther & Us

One chilly fall afternoon in 1962 found me with a little extra time after classes at Indiana University in Bloomington, Indiana. I was sitting at the edge of the Showalter Fountain, in the middle of campus, feeling a bit lonely being away from home for the first time in my young life for such a sustained period. One building skirting the fountain was the Lilly Library, named after Eli Lilly of pharmaceutical fame. I had heard there was a display of a Gutenberg Bible in the library. So, to kill time, I transferred my attention from the plumage of colorful campus foliage to the gilded leaves of the master printer's Bible. It was a moment of enlightenment and impression in my life. Some would even call it a spiritual epiphany.

It is amazing how many centuries Scripture was chained to pulpits. Not so much in order to keep the people in darkness, as to protect something so rare and precious and of great value. The masses had to take the words of their spiritual leaders as truth. Most could not even read had they owned a copy of the Bible. Now, with the inventing of the printing press and moveable type, Gutenberg was able to begin a journey of spiritual enlightenment that is with us to this day. And I wonder, genuinely wonder, if the Reformation were possible had it not been for Gutenberg. Just think of it. Gutenberg made Luther possible. No Gutenberg, no Luther! No Gutenberg, no Reformation.

There was a diabolical curse attached to the freeing of the Word of God from the churches. It seems almost anathema to suggest that the dispersing of Scripture added to the religious division in the world. One would think the opposite. One would suppose that if everyone had access to the Word, nobody could promote his own personal and pet doctrines. It would allow us to check out every heretic and expose them for what they are. But, alas, the plethora of cults and factions and sects and isms that have resulted since the printed page bear testimony to the reality that the more people have access to the Word, the more opinions there will be as to what it says. And the more opinions there are to what it says, the more cheerleading for one particular brand of Christianity over another. Besides, what good are ten Bibles in every household if none of them are read?

One of our modern day polemics has been the promotion of the idea that we can have unity based upon God's Word alone. It is a myth of recent vintage. The Word of God is the sword of the Spirit. The Word of God guides us to the Savior and salvation. The Word of God introduces us to the Person in whom we have our unity, but it does not cause the unity itself. As a matter of fact, the Word is used as the primary excuse for all of our factions. Who knows of a Christian cult or sect that does not find its origin in Scripture? So, no, unity is not in the Word of God. Unity is in the relationship we have with Jesus Christ our Lord. And if we are walking with Him in the light of His revelation, we are one in Christ. If we are out of step with Him, we are out of fellowship with each other.

Everyone of us knows we disagree on some matters of doctrine on occasion. Does this disagreement destroy our unity of the Spirit? Of course not. That would result in the cause of unity being in our ability to agree on every matter in the Bible. There aren't two scholars among us who agree on every doctrinal matter in the Scriptures. Since the appearance of the printed page, more religious division has ensued than in all of the previous history of God dealing with His people. Without the printed page, we would not even know about any Restoration movement that called for a uniting of the sects and schisms.

Are there more heretics today than there were before Gutenberg? Probably. Yet, without access to the word we have no hope. So, perhaps more than any other, Gutenberg is among our greatest preachers. For through his printed pages of Holy Writ we have come to know of our estrangement from God and how we can be reconciled. It was providence and wisdom that allowed the first printed book to be the Holy Word of God. Praise Him!

"$25 For Nothing?!"

It's heartwarming what parents will do for their children. They will stroke them and encourage them and let them think they are the greatest kids in the world. My sister and I had parents like that. It felt good to be loved so much. They were proud of our juvenile accomplishments. They bragged on handiwork that many children could have done much better. We were special.

My freshman year at Indiana University found me, against my intial wishes, in opera workshop. The music school staged full operatic productions with complete sets. It was like a mini-Metropolitan Opera. We would do two productions on Friday and Saturday evenings for three weeks. While doing those, we were learning another opera. Senior voice majors usually got the solo parts. But I was lucky. In my freshman year, I was given a solo part in *La Bohème*, Puccini's tragic masterpiece.

Occasionally we took our best productions on the road. *La Bohème* was scheduled to play in Indianapolis at one of the local high schools. I let my father know I would expect him to be at the affair with my stepmother. The tickets were pretty steep, especially for the early sixties. I know Dad had second thoughts about spending $12.50 a piece for tickets to see an opera. He was more into Hank Williams and Little Jimmy Dickens than arias sung by collegiate divas. But there he was with Lucy, sitting on the second row, waiting to see how his money for college was being used.

Of course, what I failed to tell Dad was that I had a minor (supporting) role. Jan Klopper, a male graduate organ major, and I were playing the roles of guards at the gate to the city of Paris. We were to inspect the baskets that the peasants were carrying. (I have no idea what we were expecting to find in those baskets.) But Jan's part was to sing, "Hey! What's in the basket?" I responded with all of the operatic bravado I could muster for a 120 pound tenor, "Nothing!" Then Klopper would respond with, "Pass it!" Let's cover that again one more time.

Here I was, a voice major no less, and here was Jan Klopper, an organ major, getting seven words to my one. Can you believe that? I only had one word to sing in the entire opera (besides being in the chorus, of course). "Hey! What's in the basket?" "**Nothing!**" "Pass it."

Yes, it was a sad state of affairs. I must have looked pretty sheepish shuffeling over to my folks after the production. "Hi, Dad. Hi, Lucy." Silence. "Hey, thanks a lot for coming. I really appreciate it." More silence. "How did you like the opera?" Ear deafening silence. Finally, I got up the courage, or maybe it was stupidity, and asked, "Well, Dad, did you hear my part? Did you see me? Could you hear me?" "Twenty-five dollars! I spent $25 for 'Nothing'?" Silence. "I came here and spent twenty-five hard earned dollars for '**Nothing**'?!" "Sorry, Dad, but I didn't have the heart to tell you I only had one word to sing. I thought you wouldn't come."

A smile came over Dad's face. He got me! He wasn't there because I had a solo. He wasn't there because my name was on the program as a supporting singer. He wasn't there encouraging his son to keep on seeking a career in music. He was there for the same reason he showed up at those silly grade school productions. He was there for the same reason he had come to all my choir musicals. He and Lucy were there because I was the greatest son in the world to them. They were there because they loved me, and they would have been in attendance if the tickets were $50 a piece and I had no solo.

They didn't come to my big Indianapolis debut to hear the next Luciano Pavarotti. They didn't come for "nothing." They were there for *something*, something too important to put down in words, something words can't adequately express. They were there to lend encouragement and support and love to a kid who would soon be leaving the nest forever. They were helping all of us arrange for precious memories in advance. And I thank God for the day my father paid $25 for "Nothing."

Fathers are like that. And it is no accident that God identifies Himself as our Father. He cares for all those little things we do, no matter how small they be. He wants us to excel and do well. And, like loving earthly fathers, He never misses a performance.

Jackie's Boyfriends

Sisters surely take a lot of abuse from their brothers. Since I was Jackie's little brother, I heaped as much abuse on her as I could get by with, and not lose my head. It's amazing how siblings ignore the attributes of one another. To me, my sister wasn't especially attractive. On a scale of 1 to 10 she might have registered a minus 5 in my book. Of course, I judged her looks on whether or not *I* found her attractive. Yipes! The very thought of a kid brother finding his sister a thing of beauty causes me to shudder. The boys at church and at school and in the neighborhood, however, must have thought she was a 10. I guess, from this vantage point, I suppose she probably was a 10. I just didn't know it at the time.

For some reason, my sister developed early in life. She had all the attributes for which other girls would later pay doctors or beauticians in efforts to achieve. She had dark, curly hair, blue eyes, long lashes, and those feminine curves in all the right places. I interpreted all that extra skin as fat, but the other boys saw it in another light. She was busting out all over, long before the season of her life should have begun. And the fellows took note.

It's hard for a girl to have so many suitors. I mean, how does she decide which one to give her time to in any given week? Early on, my father and mother made such decisions. What was amazing was that usually my sister liked the one or two boys who didn't seem to find her appealing. We occasionally would tease her by saying things like, "Oh, is that Norman pulling up in the driveway?" Dad or I would ask this question loud enough for Jackie to hear. Of course, Norman was the fellow she thought was the greatest thing to happen to planet earth since sliced bologna. She would rush to the window and look out and then express her displeasure with the fact that Norman wasn't within miles of our house. We got a big laugh at her expense. Sorry, Jackie.

Jackie's chasing the boys who didn't pursue her, instead of being satisfied with the many who did, always seemed to me to reaffirm that unwritten, and almost diabolical advice, that one is better off playing hard to get than in expressing her true feelings, especially in regard to romance. So there we were, a family with a path beaten to our door by paramours of the male persuasion seeking the company of one of the most popular girls in the neighborhood. Of course, Dad and Mom preferred the boys from church over those pagan fellows from high school. But, occasionally, one or two of those heathens would slip through the screening system.

Why is it that sisters will treat you like dirt and call you names and push you and slap you, but if anyone else tries it, they will defend you to their death? Jackie was my defender, being my senior and all. She was bigger than I. She was tall for her age and the boys had to work hard at catching up. Most didn't until they were in high school. I think Sis was the tallest one in her grade school graduating class. Anyway, I got tired of her calling me shrimp and creep and dodo brain. She usually hurled these monikers at me when a boy was expected to visit our domain. She would warn me, "Now, listen, Shrimp, and listen good. I don't want to see your face when Ricky gets here. Do you understand?"

When Ricky arrived (or Bill or Jim or Freddie or Rex or Tom), I usually parked myself close by so I could hear the silly talk. Sometimes the talk got downright mushy. You know what I mean, that sickening cooing between two people who think they have fallen "in like" with each other. So there I was. If they were trying to watch TV, I was also interested in what-ever was on the tube. If they wanted to sit on the porch swing, I suddenly developed an interest in outside activities. No won-der poor Jackie was always trying to make me disappear.

I've got to hand it to my sister. She usually didn't give her attention to just any guy who came around. She had pretty good taste in boyfriends, most of the time. But there was this one fellow she entertained who had the strangest tics. He would snort like a pig. I think he had some sort of allergies. He would snort real loud and then jerk his head to the side like trying to get rid of a fly on his nose without using his hands. And his hair was always a mess. It looked like a road map. He used too much greasy kid stuff on it and always looked slippery to me. She finally realized that he wasn't potential material for the future, for he was soon dispatched and replaced by the gentleman who later became my brother-in-law. Welcome to the Goad clan, Jerry!

I learned a lot while gazing at the behavior of my sister and her boyfriends. Mostly, I learned what *not* to do if ever I got a chance to date someone of the opposite sex. And I did. But I tried hard to find girls who didn't have a little brother. Know what I mean?

Chapter Four

Journeys to Maturity

A Lamb of God

It was my lot to be thrown together with this older brother in Christ. We were both attempting to use what little talents God had granted us. I was still struggling to find whatever talent it was that I might have to share. Bill had already discovered his. On casual observation one might easily have made a big mistake about the talents Bill had. On the surface it may have appeared that he was a one-talented disciple. But on closer observation, it was easy to see that this kind old gentleman was multitalented. Yet, his talents were used in areas of less profile than say, some glib pulpiteer. Bill wasn't the least concerned about getting credit for his good deeds. He was extremely unassuming. Whenever someone pointed out something good Bill had done, he was always embarrassed about it.

Bill was a lamb of a fellow. Gentle. Mild mannered. Always courteous and polite. He had a ready smile. Most people called him brother Lamb. Few called him Bill. I, especially, felt uncomfortable calling him "Bill" since I was in my early twenties and he was in his late sixties. But, he took a liking to me and insisted I call him "Bill." In the church directory, under his picture, was the name "William J. Lamb." I still have the Bible he gave to me before I went off to my first full-time church work.

Bill literally marched to the cadence of a different percussionist. He was a confirmed bachelor. I never got to look into his closet, but I would guess he had only one suit. It was black. He lived in a small apartment on the second floor of a house. He didn't have a car, nor did he have a telephone. When I first met him, he gave me the impression of being very poor. But this wasn't the case, for he had been employed at the same company for many years and had retired with full pension. What gave the impression of poverty was his stewardship of money.

One chilly fall day, Bill and I were visiting someone who had attended the services of the church. She was a middle-aged woman who had expressed a desire to study the Bible. When we arrived at her house, it must have been 50 degrees inside. She had been sitting on her couch, wearing a winter coat, covered with a thick blanket. In our brief visit we discovered that her gas had been turned off, as well as her electricity. It was at this occasion that I began developing my deep respect for Bill.

Rather than small talk, which I was inclined to do, Bill cut directly to the issue at hand. He asked, "How long have you been without heat?" She indicated that it had been off for three days. Bill asked if he could have her permission to call the gas company and power company to have her utilities restored. Then Bill asked, "Do you have any food in the house?" She handed him a grocery list that she had just made out, hoping to fill it when her disability check arrived (it was late). Bill stood up and told the woman, "We'll go to the store for you and be right back."

The grocery list was pathetic by my standards. On It was listed: milk, flour, vegetables, fruit, bathroom tissue, and "cat food." I smugly said to Bill, "We don't need to be buying cat food when this lady is hungry." Bill said nothing. I pushed the cart as he gathered the various items. He bought her several things that weren't on the list, hoping she could eat a little better than usual for a few days. I followed him to the pet food section. He put five cans of cat food in the cart. He bought the best cat food he could find. And I said nothing. He was a living sermon being preached right before my eyes. I was ashamed and awed. I asked, "Who's going to pay for all of this?"

"I am," he said simply.

We arrived back at the woman's house. She expressed embarrassment that she could not offer us something to drink or to eat. The expression on her face as we helped her put up the groceries was touching. Her face said volumes, and it provided thanks far more than words could have. She was touched and told us that nobody had ever done for her anything quite like that before. Somehow, I got the feeling this was standard procedure for Bill.

As we were putting up the last of the groceries, she looked surprised when she saw the cat food. "Why did you buy cat food?" she asked.

Bill said, "Wasn't it on the list?"

"I don't think so," she replied. "I don't have a cat."

We looked again at the list. What she was doing when we had first arrived was making up a budget for the week. The grocery list was scrawled out in an awkward cursive. She apologized for her handwriting, pointing out that she was shivering while making the list. At the bottom of the list of groceries she had written "Cab fare." But to Bill and me it looked like "Cat food." At least it looked more like "cat food" than "cab fare." We all got a laugh out of it. Yes, Bill asked how much cab fare she needed. He pulled out his checkbook and wrote out a check for the amount. She reluctantly accepted his generosity. He gave it without being sanctimonious or condescending.

As Bill wrote out the check for cab fare, I noticed a few of his ledger entries. His entry for the day's church contribution was visible. It was a figure I would not have guessed in a hundred years. Far more than I was giving. "No wonder he couldn't afford a car or nicer clothes," I thought to myself. Another entry was for the visiting missionary who had been to our services making an appeal for financial assistance. Before me was a man who literally spent most of his wages to help others. He barely saved enough for his own care.

God spoke to me through William J. Lamb. Brother Lamb couldn't say an eloquent prayer at church had he been asked to lead in prayer, which wasn't often. He certainly could not have given a talk before an audience. He couldn't carry a melody when songs were offered, but he sure could make a joyful noise unto the Lord. Bill was probably so much like Jesus that he could be lost in a crowd and nobody would recognize him. He was nondescript. Short. Bald. Bespectacled. Plain. But, oh, what a saint he was in the eyes of one younger brother.

I've met many a talented individual in my life as a minister of the gospel. I have befriended the gifted among us. I count among my friends some of the greatest gospel preachers of the 20th century. But I do not remember when I have been in the company of a man who made me any more aware of the presence of the Lord than when I was with my friend, Bill Lamb. Oh, yes, I almost forgot to tell you. The woman we visited that day accepted Christ and obeyed the gospel.

Bill's name will probably never grace a library building at one of our Christian universities. He will not be listed in Who's Who among the shakers and the leaders among men. I doubt that Bill will receive any more than the meager summary that the local paper's obituary will allow. But, one thing I know, when I was with William J. Lamb, I was in the presence of royalty. And if there are prime seats in heaven, I'm sure Bill will have a spot on the 50 yard line. And I'll be grateful just to have an upper deck seat in the same stadium.

It was Bill who first taught me what it was like to become a living sacrifice for the Lord. After being with him that day when we helped the woman in distress, I went home and took out my checkbook and glanced at the entries in the ledger. Once again, I was ashamed. It is amazing what we have decided are necessities. My spending, in relationship to Bill's, was terribly self-centered. I don't remember ever hearing a sermon that was of greater importance to me than the lesson I "heard" that Sunday afternoon with Bill. He wasn't aware that he was preaching. But, oh, what a sermon it was. And I honor him for it.

Humble Pie

Why is it that getting behind the wheel of a car can change an otherwise charming gentleman into a raving maniac? It is a Jekyll and Hyde transformation with some people. Normally I am the affable and gregarious fellow who warms the hearts of those I encounter. But on one Sunday evening my life took a turn for the worse. At least a turn was involved.

My wife and I were on our way to visit with my folks that memorable Sunday evening. We were headed for their church house for evening assembly. As we were approaching the street on which their meeting place was located, a man driving a very expensive car cut me off by turning in front of me, almost clipping my bumper. He would have hit me had I not been such a skillful driver, slamming on my brakes.

How could people be so thoughtless and careless? I was enraged. Of course, since I was in my early twenties, it didn't take a great deal to inflame my righteous indignation (this time it was more like unrighteous indignation). Why such a buffoon as this man could drive so carelessly and endanger the lives of young people like my wife and me was hard to comprehend.

I sought immediately to rectify the wrong. I sped up to the offending party and honked my horn and waved my fist in the air and said some words I would later regret. I didn't swear at the man. I did what mad Christians do. I used euphemisms for swear words. I called him names that were just short of being censored by my wife. I humiliated myself by gesticulating with my hand as though I were swatting a giant horse fly. All my dear wife could say was, "Steve, don't get so upset over nothing."

"Nothing?" I fumed, hating to be rebuked by the very witness who could corroborate my right to immediate vengeance. That made matters even worse. So I sped past the man and swerved into his lane cutting him off. "There! How do you like someone trying to occupy the same space as you?" I thought.

That sort of helped calm me down, short of forcing the fellow off the road and dragging him out of his fancy car and beating him to a pulp.

At this time in my life I was working at General Motors and preaching by appointment three Sundays a month. I prided myself on being a tent-making parson. This was the only Sunday each month I was free to attend my home congregation or visit other churches. We turned into the church parking lot where my folks attended. But as I looked into my rear view mirror, I saw the car that had cut me off pulling into the parking lot behind me.

"Great," I said to my wife. "This incompetent driver is a Christian." So I drove on through the parking lot and out the exit as though I were simply turning around. I mean, I couldn't just park my car and get out and walk with this yokel into the church house. He might recognize me. He might think I was some kind of nut for yelling and screaming and shaking my fist in the air. So we drove on down the road for a few blocks, laughed at the predicament my temper had got us in, and waited until the road hog had time to enter the church building.

When we got to the parking lot, the coast was clear. We parked and went inside thinking this shameful episode in our lives was past. Wrong! Guess who was sitting right next to my parents? Yep. I mean, how could we not sit by my folks since we were there to be with them and worship together. So we sheepishly sat next to them. Dad just had to introduce us to the couple. The man was an elder at the church and happened to be an executive vice president for the large company where my wife was employed. This man was my wife's boss' boss! Of all the people in the world to show how stupid I was, it was an elder who held the power of promotion or firing of my beloved mate. Oh, the pain of stupidity. A high price is exacted from those of us who cannot keep our cool under duress.

The man was a gentler fellow than I. He shook my hand and smiled and introduced his wife. He recognized my wife from having met her at work. And he did a wonderful thing for us all. He pretended not to recognize me as the rude man who was not willing to forgive a mistake on his part. He extended grace to me for an infraction in behavior far greater than his. His was a matter of accidentally cutting me off by not having seen me. My lack of social grace was deliberate and willful and spiteful. I was red-faced with embarrassment.

This wasn't the last time I got mad behind the wheel. But it left a lasting impression on my mind that those of us who claim to be following in the footsteps of Jesus had better take our steps through life more carefully. My favorite pie had been pumpkin. I didn't like the taste of humble pie. I've had to eat it on several occasions, but that evening at church it was especially bitter.

Next time you are tempted to blow up in a fit of rage, bite your tongue, count to ten, chill out and be careful. You never know who you might be abusing. And you will know for sure the Lord isn't amused.

Matthew's Birth Day

No male had been born to a Goad as the first child as far back as any of us could remember. There were always at least two children, sometimes more, and the firstborn was invariably a girl. So, I took a sense of pride in knowing that I was the first to break with tradition, as though I had anything to do with it.

It was a cold January day in Indianapolis. Snow had covered the ground and enough of it was sticking to cause ice to form on the highways. Matthew's mother was in labor for a long time, almost eighteen hours. It was a hard delivery. But when the world welcomed my firstborn son at 4:05 a. m. that Sunday morning, he was strong and vocal, all eight pounds thirteen ounces of him. The first thing I recall seeing, besides that great head of dark black hair, were his hands. Such large and perfectly formed, delicate hands. They seemed too big for a baby's hands. And then I saw those eyes, those beautiful, deep blue eyes.

The gift of fatherhood happens with the firstborn. It is an awesome thing to have a helpless soul completely dependent upon one's self. Life can never be the same after a parent holds his own flesh and blood in his hands and realizes it is another human being, created in the image of God Himself. Matthew's appearance made me want to dance and sing and run up and down the corridors of the hospital praising my Lord. Instead, I called my father on the phone, Matthew's grandfather, and woke him up. It wasn't even 5 a.m. as I exclaimed, "Dad, it's a boy!" My father said, "It can't be." "Oh, but yes it can be," I responded. "Every first child born to a Goad has always been a girl, for as long as we can recall," Dad mused.

After seeing to it that all was well, I left the hospital and headed for home so I could get ready for church. I couldn't wait to get to the church house and tell the church secretary to include Matthew's birth in the morning announcements. She asked me to write down his weight and height and name.

I nervously wrote down: "Matthew Clark Goad, 22 inches long, 13 pounds & 8 ounces." Everyone got a big laugh at my expense when they learned that I had reversed the numbers for his weight. Let's see now. That was eight pounds and thirteen ounces. We had broken with one tradition and begun perpetuating another. Not only was I born on Sunday, but so were both of my dear sons. Mark was born during the evening worship service. It was the shortest sermon I have ever preached, and I was still fifteen minutes late to the hospital.

Through the years, I have taken a lot of ribbing for having sons named Matthew and Mark. "Oh, are you going to finish the gospels and have Luke and John?" Ha, ha, ho, ho! "No! We are going to be happy with an abridged gospel account." Tee hee!

Matthew has taught me so much about life, far more than I have taught him. He has taught me how to be less selfish. He has taught me the weighty responsibility of teaching a child about Jesus. Matthew has helped me better understand the deep love our heavenly Father has for us which He demonstrated by giving His only begotten Son in our place so that we might be saved. A parent would rather give up his own life than to surrender the lives of his children to others. My son has also helped me better understand the idea of innocence, as Jesus tells us to become like little children in order to enter the Kingdom of Heaven.

Beloved Matthew, Mark and Caitlin, how I adore them so.

His Animals

I respect them. They deserve better treatment than most of us are willing to give them. After all, they were here before we. At least, they were here before our ancestors arrived on the scene. God's creation, His living, breathing, procreating animals were given the breath of life and have occupied the planet longer than we. I call us to acknowledge that. And I call us to have some respect for these "lower" life forms which we manipulate and use too readily for our own selfish purposes.

It seems I have always talked to animals. As I plunge to the very depths of my memory, I can't recall my first such conversation, but talking to animals has given me a great sense of being. And it has given me a peace that I could not have obtained by merely talking to my fellow humans. My wife shares my love for God's creatures, in fact, even referring to them as "persons." Not that she is making a theological statement about the personhood of animals, nor that she wishes to doctrinalize the issue of animals' rights, but, rather, she does so in recognition that animals are animated beings in many ways similar to ourselves. Not biologically similar necessarily, although that is true, but similar in the sense that they are animal beings on the same order of our being human beings.

It is amazing that the same word used in the Hebrew to say that God made us living souls is used when speaking of animals becoming living beings. It's God's breath that sustains us all: humans and animals. All throughout Scripture God has used animals to teach us lessons that we couldn't seem to learn otherwise. From Balaam's donkey friend to Jonah's big fish to the sluggard's ant to the sacrifices and sin offerings, God's animal kingdom speaks to us the messages of heaven. From the den of Daniel's lions to the floating zoo of Noah, we are surrounded in Scripture with the presence of these beings. There is not a bird that dies but what the Lord takes note. Perhaps we should give more thought to how we treat these fellow creatures of the planet.

My dogs were constant auditors when I needed someone

to talk to. Amazingly, they never grew tired of my oratory. Whether I was in a good mood, or sad, they would listen intently and usually give me encouragement. That was, frankly, more than I could say for some of my fellows. Birds and squirrels would heed my meandering discourses with far greater attentiveness than some people might have in any given congregation for which I have proclaimed the word of God. Confessions to chipmunks and toads have allayed my fears on many an occasion.

The older I grow, the more difficult it is for me to eat God's creatures. I don't know that Adam or Eve ever ate an animal before the fall. Perhaps it wasn't in God's original design. I know the three Hebrew young men of fiery furnace fame would not eat of the king's meat, but ate only vegetables. They were mightier and wiser than the rest. I cannot bring myself to sport at the death of one of His beings. The letting of blood seems to me a horrendous undertaking by those of us covered by the blood of Christ. I would have hated to be the bloodletting priest who was forced by sin to smell of death and hear its silent good-bye. Jesus, both Lion and Lamb, made that kind of bloodletting obsolete.

Animals talk to me in the morning. They speak that the world is still on its axis and the sun is again where it ought to be. Roosters and horses attest to the joy of another day. Unwanted kittens sadly bemoan our need to be better stewards of God's domain. Their importance to our harmony and peace is so vital. The pets that we breed become weaker and weaker and remind us that nature's management abilities are often far superior to our own. The earth, and all that dwells within it, cries out that we treat each other better. That we take time for each other. That we stop and communicate from time to time. And so, I say "hello" to the passing sheepfold. I salute the herd of pastured cattle. I lament the captivity of the wild ones held against their wills behind bars. I sing with the sparrows and mockingbirds the glory of God's creation and long for the day when the lion shall lay down with the lamb, and the child shall play at the cobra's nest unharmed.

Behold, His wonderous animals!

Get Ready, Get Set . . .

Why is it that so many people in life never seem to learn how to do it? Life, I mean. They are always planning on doing something "one of these days." Yet, "one of these days" has never been on any calendar I have ever seen. They intend to make a trip to Hawaii or finish that college degree or write that book. Someone has well said that the road to hell is paved with good intentions. So, a lot of us end up like Pa Kettle, with chores abounding and all kinds of plans on how to get them done . . . next week. Procrastination has many of us by the throat.

When I was a young man, just married, I had decided to take on a part-time job. It was one of those jobs where you really needed a lot of self-confidence. I sold knives. Now, you couldn't ask the price we were asking for this merchandise and call them knives. As a matter of fact, "knife" was sort of a cuss word to our sales manager. We sold the world's finest *cutlery*. If you knew what we got for a set of these knives, you'd surely understand why we had to call them cutlery.

They were good knives, uh, I mean, cutlery. And I believed in my product. These kitchen utensils had three different patents. The cutting edge was patented. The metal alloy was patented. And the handle was patented. These pieces of cutlery were truly unique, and I was sold on the idea of every home in America having at least one full set. Times were tough. Sales tax had just begun in my home state. So it wasn't the best of times to be taking on an extra job, especially in sales.

Imagine, if you will, the obstacles I had to overcome. Most of our leads were young women who were thinking of marriage. Though we also sold to housewives, unmarried young ladies were prime candidates for owning our cutlery. So I had to give a demonstration of why each young lady needed a complete set of our cutlery in her hope chest. My demonstration was powerful and persuasive. I had to admit it, I had the routine down to a tee. I even cut a penny in half with the free kitchen shears that I would throw in with the set if the customer bought on the spot. And I gave away a kitchen tool set with the famous patented handles, just to show my appreciation. And I was good. And I was sales leader.

Selling knives, I mean, cutlery, was a challenge. When our hot leads were all used up, we had to cold door knock to get someone to allow us to make a demonstration. We had a knife that was one of the favorites in all of the set. It was a kitchen slicing knife. So we salesmen bought several of these and would leave them at homes for a week and ask the lady of the house to try it and let us know how she liked it when we came calling again. Think, for a moment, of what we had to do. We had to knock on the door of homes with a knife in our hand. Can you imagine doing that in LA today, or any place else for that matter? But I sold a few knives, I mean, cutlery, to women who tried my kitchen slicer.

I was so good (my modesty is embarrassing) that I won a trip to the company convention. It was one of those pep rally type affairs where we were urged to keep the faith and not grow weary in well doing. There were thousands of us at that convention. Speech after speech. Lecture after lecture. I got bored. So instead of listening to how I could learn some new technique, I demonstrated my cutlery for a waitress in a restaurant where I was eating. She bought the entire set and paid me cash for it. My boss was impressed. When he gave his speech, he used me as an example of determination, although he was a little embarassed that I had skipped the speeches to make a sale.

Guess what? God doesn't care about what we are going to do some day. He wants our attention today! He isn't so much impressed about our potential as He is with our delivery of what we now possess. One thing I've learned about life, whether it is selling knives or sharing Jesus, the sale is made in the excellent demonstration. God wants us to demonstrate our discipleship. Talking about holiness may have its place, but living holiness is far better. I sold cars for a few years, too. Guess what? Nobody bought a car while he was kicking tires. But when I got customers into cars and demonstrated their features, I sold a lot more of them.

I was at Pepperdine University for the annual April lectureship. I love the lectureships at Pepperdine. The locale has got to be one of the premier campuses in America for sheer beauty. Rolling real estate overlooks the gorgeous Pacific Ocean at Malibu. As a minister of Christ I have attended all sorts of workshops and seminars and lectureships. On occasion I would feel guilty leaving my work at home and going away to talk about being holy and discuss how to evangelize. Sometimes it occurred to me that staying home and evangelizing might be a lot more productive. But I counted these occasions as brief sabbaticals in which I renewed my vows to God and my fellows to share my faith with others.

Anyway, I was enjoying the lectures and classes on campus. During the second day of the event, I met a young sophomore in the dining room. What a picturesque place to have lunch, with its panoramic view of the Pacific. The young man sat across from me. He reminded me a little of my son, Matthew. So I initiated a conversation. "Are you here for the lectures?" I asked.

"No," he replied. "I'm a student finishing up my sophomore year." He had been working at the campus as a helper during the lectureship. The campus is actually empty of students in the normal sense during lectures. It's the first week after classes are dismissed that the lectureship is scheduled. So this young man, his name was Tim, was making some extra money by assisting in various capacities.

Our conversation shifted to what was happening on campus. He asked me about the lectureship. He discovered I was a minister of the gospel. I was delighted in his eagerness to find out about Pepperdine's beginnings, as well as the churches of Christ. I took the opportunity to briefly tell him what I knew about George Pepperdine. I also answered his several questions about the churches of Christ. I gave Tim a thumbnail sketch of the Restoration plea and how we were attempting to be undenominational in our approach to Christianity. He was fascinated beyond the time I had to answer all his questions. So I asked if he could meet me that day, or the next, for more conversation. We scheduled a time.

The next day, Tim brought his Bible with him. I hadn't even told him to. He happened to be Presbyterian insofar that he had been brought up in that denomination. I shared the ties that the Campbells had with Presbyterianism and how they were players in the unfolding of a pioneer American movement that culminated in what our fellowship was all about. He was intrigued. As we were studying, I selfishly thought of how many classes and main lectures I was missing. After all, I had come to Pepperdine to get my spiritual batteries charged. I chose to stay with Tim for as long as his interest lasted. I still got a charge.

On the third day of our study, I shared the gospel plan of salvation with Tim. He seemed thrilled that someone would take the time to share Christ with him. I told him that there were several on campus who could have done just that. He eagerly accepted Christ and we prepared to have him baptized in the Runnels swimming pool on campus. Author Billie Silvey and I found the campus minister who assisted in the actual baptism. Tim's obeying the gospel made that my best lectureship ever.

I share these stories to remind us that life is right under our noses and we miss it. It's sort of like that man in "Acres of Diamonds" who had been living on one of the largest diamond fields as a young man but went away to seek his fortune elsewhere. It reminds me of the woman who took the whirlwind trip to all the "must see" sights in Europe. When she got home, a friend asked her how Paris was and whether she got to see the Eiffel Tower. "Paris?" the woman began. "Oh, yes, Paris. That's where I spilled wine on my new red dress."

Excuse me, but too many of us are in such a hurry to get to our destinations that we don't take time to enjoy the beauty of the trip along the way. It's trite and schmaltzy, but the roses are blooming and we are often too busy pulling weeds. We go to conventions and miss sales opportunities. We talk about Christianity while souls are right beside us who need to hear the message of a Savior. Maybe these stories are reminders once again for us not to be in such a rush to arrive at our destination that we miss the joys of the journey. And maybe these stories will help us not to overlook possibilities that stare us in the face while we are looking the other way. I mean, if a man can stand in the doorway of homes with a knife in his hand and make a living at it, just imagine the other possibilities.

Get ready. Get set. Live.

Chapter Five

Journeying with Jesus

An Imitator of Christ

I was in my second full-time ministry as the "pulpit preacher" for a splendid church in Southern Indiana. It was a wonderful fellowship, one that I regretted leaving immediately, right from the day the moving van pulled out of town with our belongings headed for Mobile, Alabama.

There was a spirit to save the lost within so many of those who made up that marvelous Indiana congregation. We had the evangelistic fire. We were in the top 3% of churches in number of baptisms per member. Our elders were mission-minded. Our growth had prompted a building program and move into a new, beautiful facility. It was then that he showed up at one of our assemblies. His name was Dan Keeran.

Rich Little always captivated my attention. I would love it

when he did Jimmy Stewart or John Wayne. He could even do Cary Grant, Georgie Jessel and Johnny Carson. My favorite was Jack Benny. When I closed my eyes and listened to Rich Little imitate Jack Benny I would "affirm" it was actually Benny doing the talking. Little is the consummate mimic. He does magnificent impressions of celebrities. His fame came about by imitating those who were truly famous. Ironic, isn't it?

Dan Keeran probably didn't realize he was a mimic, too. When he arrived on the scene, he seemed different. He looked different. He behaved differently. And some were suspicious of him. I admit it, I was a bit suspicious, too. But I opened my hand of fellowship to him and we became great friends. What made Dan so glaringly different from the rest of us is that he was attempting to be an imitator of Christ to a degree that shamed and embarrassed even those of us who, heretofore, were deeming ourselves as true 20th century Christians. Let me explain.

Brother Keeran was close to my age. We were both in our early 30s. He was educated. I think he had a Masters degree in social work. And he was a social worker. He served in that capacity in Louisville, Kentucky, just across the Ohio River from us. He drove an old jalopy that looked like it had been through two world wars plus Vietnam. His hair was down to his shoulders and his clothes were borderline Goodwill rejects. But he had a smile a mile wide and everyone soon learned to love him.

As we had Dan into our home, we learned more about him. He didn't have a bed. He didn't have a phone. He didn't have much of a wardrobe (two or three changes of clothes). You would think by a superficial glance that he was a street person. He had one spoon and one fork and one knife. I think he only had one plate and one bowl and one cup. He was a rarity in Christianity of modern vintage. He was an ascetic. It was a matter of principle with him.

I used to kid him about enjoying eating at my table while not having a table himself to share in hospitality with me. He said he didn't need to own a table to extend hospitality. And he was right. I chided him for not having any pictures on his walls and how sad it was he didn't have a couch to enjoy, like the one he was sitting on in my living room as we visited. He said that those who visited him sat where he sat, on the floor. And he was right.

It is amazing how we are threatened when we observe those doing what we suspect might be a better job of discipleship than we. We challenge their resolve. We think up scenarios that are supposed to show the futility of their behavior. I remember asking Dan how he could depend upon a car that was so old and so worn out. He explained that it would cost less for him to buy another car than it would for me to buy a new part for my late model vehicle. And he was right.

Dan met and married his wife while at our congregation before soon moving to another city. Before his wedding, I advised him that he might be forced to alter his lifestyle, that taking on a mate might require him to purchase entire sets of china and flatware. I even hinted that she might expect him to at least get a mattress, even if he didn't want to spend money on an actual bed. He good naturedly patronized my ignorance.

I wondered what Dan did with his money. Being the nosy type, I asked him. And, of course, he had a good answer for me. He would take his vacation time, and money, and go to poverty stricken areas, in such places as Mexico, and stay there and help them build a baptistery or a small shelter for assembly. He literally paid for the trips and the construction expenses with his own money. Without fanfare. Without applause. Except maybe from heaven.

A few of the folk at church thought Dan had taken the business of imitating Christ to a fanatical extreme. After getting to know him, I decided he hadn't. I decided he was a living rebuke to those of us who haven't yet learned how to be genuinely frugal. I discovered that Dan was able to divest himself of the trappings that we have decided are necessities. It is amazing that about 95 percent of the "necessities" we now enjoy were not available just a century ago. Dan, to me, was a modern day John the Baptist. His presence in my life made me painfully aware of how much control "things" had wielded in my life. He taught me a dimension of stewardship that I hadn't known existed, except in theory.

One day, while I was in one of my sanctimonious moods and looking for a loophole in brother Keeran's lifestyle, I asked him why he didn't get his hair cut. He said it was useless to cut his hair because it cost money and would grow back anyway. And he was right. And he reminded me that many Biblical characters didn't cut their hair and were pleasing to God. And when he did get a hair cut, it was when some kind brother offered to do so with his own clippers.

One evening, while this vagabond of God sat at my table in my air-conditioned house eating my food with my silverware on my plate in my hardrock maple chair, I mentioned in passing that our family was experiencing some financial stresses at that moment. Our bills had exceeded our income for too many months and we were in a spot. I wasn't telling him this to garner his sympathy, and I surely wasn't telling him this in order to ask for money. The thought had never crossed my mind that he would even consider giving us money, we, who wasted so much of it on furniture and chairs and flatware and such. We, who threw money to the wind buying late model cars. We, who had two TV's and two cars and two boys. But Dan did a very unexpected thing. He asked me, "How much money do you need?" And while asking, he pulled out his checkbook and prepared to write in the stated amount. Not a loan. It would have been a gift. He insisted we take it. I declined.

I don't know to this day if I did the right thing. It is often an insult to refuse a gift genuinely offered by one who loves you. Dan loved us as much as we loved him. And in my eagerness to find some chink in his armor, always goading him about his bare-bones lifestyle, it never occurred to me that he did not once suggest that I was a poor steward. He did not once judge my motivation for having too many suits and one too many late model cars. He had accepted me where I was and for who I was. And in doing so, he genuinely was an imitator of Christ.

There haven't been all that many Dan Keerans in my life.

I learned important truths about stewardship from my scruffy Christian friend. We are so ensconced in materialism and worldliness that I doubt many of us are even aware of how much we do waste. Dan taught me how to better share what I have and not to put so much trust in the things of this world.

Burial at Sea?

Everyone knew her as "Bootsie." She was a hefty, jovial lady of middle age who had been taught by one of my all time favorite elders in the church. This elder was especially dear to me because of his evangelistic spirit. He was so eager to teach the lost that he went on campaigns during his vacation time off. Now, that is the kind of elder who is genuinely an encouragement to an evangelist.

Not only was this dear elder evangelistic, he was one of the most nervous people I have ever met. He was generally so befuddled, he could literally get lost in a grocery store. We won't even mention his driving habits. Once, while he was giving announcements, he decided he had lost his notes. He fumbled and peeked and poked in every pocket in what would seem like a comedic routine to anyone who didn't know Frank. Meanwhile, his notes were in his hand. What a marvelous soul.

Anyway, Bootsie was finally ready to obey the gospel. But there was one thing that gave her pause about being baptized; she was deathly afraid of water. She had never learned to swim for that reason. She was claustrophobic even in the bathtub (she only took showers).

There we were, ready for the baptism. Several friends and relatives had gathered to witness the precious occasion. As always, I encouraged the one who had done the teaching to perform the baptism. I sort of felt like Paul did when he said, "I thank God that I baptized none of you except Crispus and Gaius." For some reason I never developed what many preachers seem to crave, the excitement of donning waders and raising hands in the air to assist those being baptized. It only seemed natural to me that the one who taught the lost soul should be the one to do the delivery. I always birthed the disciples I taught.

Frank found himself, nervous as he was, the man on the spot to baptize this aqua-challenged believer. It took us quite some time to even talk her into stepping down into the baptistery. She was there with hanky in hand ready for whatever was about to occur. Frank raised his hand high in the air and said some words that pretty well fit the occasion. Then it happened. It was more like a drowning than a baptism. Frank grabbed Bootsie by her throat and pushed her backwards, burying her head under water while her frame floated on top. Frank got nervous and didn't know what to do. I yelled, "Let her up!" He, reluctantly, realizing that she hadn't been properly buried, allowed her head to come up out of the water. She had been clawing and grabbing the sides of the baptistery with her hands all the while. She came up out of the water sputtering and choking. We sat her down on the steps. She started to cry. I felt sorry for her. "Whatever shall we do?" I thought. Did Philip have this sort of problem with the eunuch?

After several moments of coaching and encouraging her, and after very specific instructions to Frank on how to baptize someone the size of Bootsie, we had a prayer and attempted the baptism once again. Like taking a Boy Scout oath, Frank held his hand up in the air once more to recite whatever it was he had said earlier. I suggested that we didn't have to do that again and he quickly agreed. So he proceeded to nervously lower Bootsie back into the water. Once again her torso floated to the top. It was worse than the first time. Frank got even more nervous. He lifted a leg and tried to push her body down with his knee, appearing to be attempting to get on top of her. There was a hush in the small assembly. "Let her up!" I yelled, even more loudly this time. I have never yelled at an elder before, nor have I since. I made an exception in that case.

Poor Frank raised his hand even higher this time, and once again I encouraged him not to by saying, "Why don't we just do it?" This time Bootsie kept her feet on the floor of the baptistery as she was instructed. This time Frank had her fold her hands and cup her face and hold her nose and lean back into his hand. This time I was there to facilitate the management of any parts of her anatomy that might surface before the immersion was completed. What had to me always been such an easy task had become a major undertaking. But, thanks to the grace of God and the willingness of a new believer, we were able to accomplish once again that new birth that Jesus spoke of to Nicodemus. But I shall never forget the day a death and burial almost occurred without that corresponding resurrection.

"She Just Quit"

She had attended the church for a little over two years, along with her two young children. No one knew if she had a husband or not, because they didn't ask. As a matter of fact, nobody knew much of anything about this sister in Christ because they never took the time to get acquainted with her. Oh, they offered the usual "How are you's" in the church foyer after services, but no real concern for her was evident. She suddenly quit attending the worship services. Few missed her.

It occurred to one member of the church that someone was missing from the usual make-up of the congregation. Who could it be? By thinking long and hard, it became apparent that one young mother with the cheerful smile was not sitting in her normal place in the auditorium. "Let's see. What was her name?" The member asked others if they could recall the name of the slender brunette who had not been to worship for several weeks. Or had it been months? Someone thought to look at the picture board. Sure enough, her picture, along with her two little girls, had been taken and included in the pictorial board. Smith. "Yes, that was her name. Barbara Smith."

A few members began to discuss Barbara Smith and one concluded that she must have moved, or worse, just quit coming.

"You know, I see a lot of people here for a while, and then they just disappear. I wonder what could be wrong? They just quit coming to church."

Let me share with you one case history of the myriads that come and go in the thousands of churches across the land. This is the story of one of those mysterious souls who appeared for a little while and then vanished away.

Yes, her name "was" Barbara Smith. Yes, she had two little girls. No, she didn't have a husband. He deserted her and the girls when he decided he loved his secretary more than he loved his wife. Yes, Barbara had attended the church from the very first week she moved into town. She had grown up in the church. She had been faithful in attendance for two years, four months and one week. She was at every Bible class on Sunday and every morning worship service except when ill. She was unable to attend Sunday evening services because of her work, but nobody knew that. Nobody asked her about that. She occasionally attended Wednesday evening services when her work didn't conflict.

What were the children's names? No one remembered. They weren't even on the picture that was posted. Did Barbara just quit church one day? Did she just wake up one morning and say to herself, "I think I'll stop loving Jesus today. I think I'll just quit Bible class and worship and find better things to do with my time and with my girls"? No, indeed. Here is why Barbara Smith no longer attends a church full of people whose lives were too busy and too full to notice her and her girls.

Barbara wasn't the best dressed member of the church. Perhaps a few made wrong judgments about her from the first day she arrived. But sister Smith was always clean and her girls were, too. She was a bit shy and somehow managed to find a place to sit in the back two or three rows of pews. When she first came to church people greeted her with all the normal expressions of welcome.

"Nice to have you here. Are you from town or just moved in? We hope you'll come back and be with us again."

And these greetings were probably well intended. Somewhere along the way, Barbara's presence seemed to have been taken for granted. After the first few formalities were observed, little interest in Barbara and her girls was evident. A"Hi!" or maybe a "How ya' doin'?" was about it.

Barbara's faithfulness in attendance seemed not to lag in spite of the lack of hospitality extended. Nobody had asked her to their home. Nobody had sent get-well cards when the girls got sick, even though their names were on the sick list. Nine months into her attendance, Barbara became ill. She underwent exploratory surgery. A tumor was found. It was cancer. Surgery and chemo treatments found her missing sporadically. Nobody noticed. Her hospitalization was announced at church and in the bulletin. A generic prayer was offered for the sick. Barbara never found out she was prayed for. All she knew was that nobody offered to help with the girls. Nobody sent her a get-well card. Nobody visited her in the hospital. Nobody offered to be her friend or to have her girls over to play with their children. Nobody came by her home to welcome her to the community and to the church. Few noticed she was at church. Nobody cared.

"Did you ever find out about what happend to that Barbara Smith with the two little girls?"

"Not really. I looked up her name in the phone directory and couldn't find it. I called the church secretary and she said she had never been able to get the phone number."

"Well, what do you think happend?"

"I think she was probably someone who was not very faithful in the first place and just decided to quit. You know the kind?"

Oh, how wrong we can be. Barbara didn't quit the church. The church quit Barbara. And Barbara died. Oh, she may have died spiritually had she lived. But she literally died and was buried. Alone. With no support net or concern from those who should have cared the most. Her girls are in foster care. The couple from church who were eager to adopt two children under the ages of 10 would have been happy to have had Barbara's children. But they will never know. Nobody will ever know. But God knows. I wonder how many Barbaras come and go among us and never become a part of us?

Complacency. Indifference. Self-centeredness. What malignant sins these are. They lie hidden, like a cancer, in churches all over the world. Drunks are easily noticed in a holy fellowship. Liars and thieves and drug addicts are often exposed. But who will expose those of us who care so little that we sometimes miss the Barbaras of this world? Of course, God will do that kind of exposing. But it will be too late for some of us.

Jim & Dorothy

We all too often take for granted the gifts of our senses. We smell and taste and listen and feel and watch without giving much thought to what we are doing. To see is one of the greatest of physical gifts. To observe a sunset or to know visually what the color green looks like instead of having to guess are blessings that those who have never had their eyesight impaired usually give no thought to. To be able to listen to the sounds of the forest, with the rustling of the leaves and the voice of the mockingbird, are experiences most of us do not find fascinating, for they are routine. Jim and Dorothy Hogan remind me of the gifts of our five senses. They only have three of their senses to work with.

Helen Keller was a marvelous individual who rose above her handicaps to become a leader among people. She had a tremendous burden to overcome: the inability to see and hear. To be deaf and blind is a horribly crippling condition. It erases from your life experience two-thirds of your sensory perception. And these two perceptions, or senses, are at the top of the scale of importance. The loss of one's sense of smell might put him in danger if a fire was raging and the smoke couldn't be noticed, but it would hardly impede one's intellectual growth. And the absence of the ability to taste might make eating a drudgery, rather than a culinary experience, but it would hardly stunt one's social graces.

Jim and Dorothy were a bright couple. They were highly intelligent and both possessed magical senses of humor (perhaps a sixth sense that allowed them to function better than some with all of their faculties intact). Faithful Christians, Jim and Dorothy rarely missed a church assembly, and then only if one was bedfast. Their devotion to each other was legend and made other couples with domestic problems seem almost ashamed of themselves when they got to having a pity party. After all, look how happy the Hogans were, in spite of their misfortune. They, of course, didn't look to their twin conditions as misfortunes. The Hogans were blind and deaf.

I became close friends with Jim and Dorothy. My wife and I were able to speak to them by signing in their hands, just as Anne Sullivan had done with Helen Keller. We had learned sign language years before, and it surely came in handy when we met the Hogans. All of my sermons were typed out on a Braille typewriter by my wife so they could follow along as they sat, in silence, in our assembly. The church had purchased a Braille typewriter so we could prepare sermons and type the words to all of the songs in our song book. Before assemblies, the song leader would call us and give us his selection of songs. After a while we had almost all of the songs in our book typed in Braille. They were given the exact song the congregation was singing at any given time. So, in their silence, they were able to sing with us. And I am still amazed at those of us who will not so much as make a joyful noise unto the Lord.

Jim and Dorothy were our unofficial greeters at church. They were usually among the first to arrive and the last to leave. They enjoyed their holy hugs more than anything and would make you feel special whether you could sign to them or not.

One other thing I recall about this wonderful example of rising above the meager hand that is sometimes dealt us, the Hogans had the most infectious smiles. You would think they had just won the *Reader's Digest* Sweepstakes, by the expressions on their precious faces.

Sometimes I get up with an ache in my back and I'm tempted to curse the darkness. Occasionally some little something will disrupt my well choreographed routine and I almost think I have serious reason to show my temper. We all have hardships at times. But few of us must live with the day-to-day challenges of Jim and Dorothy Hogan. They are a living testimony of perseverance under pressure. Their faith has helped make me a more dedicated disciple of Jesus.

The Con?

ME: "Hello."

HIM: "Is this the pastor of the church of Christ?"

ME: "No, this is Steve. May I help you?"

HIM: "Is the pastor in?"

ME: "No they're not, but I am the preacher or minister for the church. How may I help you?"

HIM: "That's what I said, Reverend."

ME: "I beg your pardon?"

HIM: "That's what I said. I asked for the pastor and you *are* the pastor, aren't you?"

ME: "No, sir. I'm the full-time minister of the word."

HIM: "Whatever."

ME: "What was it you wanted?"

HIM: "Well, I'm on my way back from my grandmother's funeral and I've had some car trouble. I was wondering if you could help me get a part for my car and maybe give me some gas money."

ME: "Are you a Christian?"

HIM: "Yes, Reverend, I am."

ME: "Where do you attend church?"

HIM: "Well, we haven't been attending much lately, but when we go, we attend the First Possum Trot Church of the Holy Sepulchre in Mealy Meal, Nebraska." (You all know I made up the name of this church, but since he made up a name of some church, I thought I might as well do it, too. Besides, I can't remember the name he gave me, or the names of any of the myriads of other churches world travelers have given me when using the church as their travel agent and financier.)

ME: "So, you aren't a member of the church of Christ?"

HIM: "That's right. But we sure do love the Lord and know that when a man is down and out all he has to do is go to where the Lord's people are and he can get help. Yes, sir!"

ME: "Can you give me the name of your minister or pastor?"

HIM: Long pause as he thinks up a name. "Uh, Bob Smith. Yes, Pastor Bob Smith is his name."

ME: "Sir, if you'll give me the name of your church again, I'll be happy to call Bob Smith long distance and ask him to wire some money to help you get out of your jam. What was the name of your church again?"

HIM: An even longer pause this time, because I just knew he forgot the name he made up the first time. Sure enough. "Uh, we attend the Second Shining Star Pentecostal Jumpin Jehosaphat Assembly of the Gathered Disciples of the Holy One Hisself, Reformed."

ME: "Sir, you wouldn't be pulling my leg would you?"

HIM: "What do you mean?"

You see, I had been taking notes the entire time. I have developed a way to ferret out con artists who prey on the church. First of all, I make it as hard as possible on them to talk me into feeling sorry for them. The way I do that is to ask lots of questions. Especially questions I can check out.

ME: "Well, you changed the name of the church where you said you occasionally attended."

HIM: Total silence. He was deciding if it was worth the effort to continue the con.

ME: "Now, who did you say your preacher was?"

HIM: "Uh, Bill Jones?"

ME: "No! I'm asking you. I don't know who your preacher is. Is it Bob Smith or Bill Jones?"

HIM: *Click! Dial tone.*

I had won the war of words. The cons had touched me one too many times. I know that we are told to help all people, even the con artists, for fear of missing the one who is in genuine need. We are encouraged to be careful how we treat people for we may be entertaining "angels without knowing it." I figure the angels don't really need the money in the first place. Surely, they have an expense account, or something like that.

RING!

ME: "Hello!"

HIM: "My name is Cletus Liptschitze. Do you help people?"

ME: "Yes, we do, Cletus. What kind of help do you need?" It was the same guy who had just called. He apparently lost track of his churches as he was checking them off in the phone book. He didn't realize he was talking to the same parson.

HIM: "We're on our way home from my grandmother's funeral and had some car trouble."

ME: "And you need us to help you get a part for the car and give you some gas money so you can get back to Nebraska, right?"

HIM: *Click! Dial tone.*

To this day I don't quite know exactly how to deal with panhandlers and freeloaders who beg from the church. I have a stewardship responsibility to God and to those who fund the local work where I minister. It is wrong to encourage people not to work. One man held up a sign that I thought was the typical "Will Work For Food" appeal, but it said, "Why lie? I need a beer." I smiled at his ingenuity, but still resisted handing him over a dollar bill. His truthfulness was appreciated, but he still was a bum who wanted a beer without working for it.

Yes, I've helped hundreds of folk "just traveling through." Some were delightful and totally honest. We have baptized a few. But ninety-nine percent of the time, these vagabonds are after the order of Melchizedek. They have no origin or beginning point. All their relatives are dead. They haven't a church affiliation. No friends can be found. No last address is given. Often they refuse to give any identification. And yet if we do not meet all their needs they often become indignant. I've been called just about every name in the book. I've had a knife pulled on me. One man pulled a gun. It wasn't loaded, but it scared the stuffing out of me.

We are to be wise as serpents and harmless as doves. But we aren't to be hard-hearted. I admit, I still feel cold and uncaring, even when I know I am being conned. Because I won't just say "Yes" to every request from the vagabonds of the world who network churches and usually are overweight.

RING! "Hello?"

HIM: "Is this the church of Christ?"

ME: "No, this is Steve."

HIM: "Oh, I was calling the church of Christ."

ME: "Well, I'm the preacher for the church of Christ."

HIM: "Yes! Hello, Pastor. I was wondering if you could help me with some food and gas money. I'm on my way to Las Vegas and I lost my wallet and identification. If you could write a cashier's check out for the requested amount I would appreciate it. Whadya say?"

ME: "Well, sir. We don't give out money to anyone, period. We haven't the resources to help all those who ask. So, what we do is provide some canned goods and offer to help you call your local church back home to see if they can wire you some help."

HIM: *Click. Dial tone.*

I've heard all the sad tales anyone can imagine. Some of the same folk have hit me on multiple occasions with the same story. One fellow had his father dying three times. The first time he got me for two tires and a full tank of gas. The next two times, I got him. He wasn't even embarrassed. Occasionally I wonder if I am missing an angel now and then.

I doubt it!

Twilight Zone Story

Rod Serling always held me captive as he would stand
with hands folded in front and grimly say something on the
order of this: "You are now entering another dimension,
another time and place, as it were. You are leaving the realm
of reality and stepping into a world where fantasy is real and
reality is fantasy. You are leaving time and space as we know
it and experiencing life . . . in the ***twilight zone***." Then the
music "*nah na nah na nah na nah na*" would begin. And chills
would fill our arms and necks with goose bumps and our hair
would seem to stand on end. What followed was a tale that
defied our sense of normalcy, but it all seemed to make sense,
at least for half an hour, because, after all, it was the *Twilight
Zone*. How Mr. Serling could talk without moving his lips was
also mysterious. The story that follows is true. Most of the
names have been omitted because I can't remember them.

It was one of those currently popular three-day church
meetings. We call them "gospel meetings" and some churches
call them "revivals" or "revival meetings." I had just conducted such a meeting in Hartford, Connecticut. This meeting
was intended to equip the saints there with some skills at
approaching people with the message of a Savior. It was a
nuts and bolts meeting with the intended purpose more to
train soul winners than to win souls. We hope both were
accomplished. Only God knows for sure. And maybe only God
knows what happened before I got home.

While on my way home, life took a turn toward the
bizarre. The wonderful Christians who had hosted my time
there had said their good-byes and left me at the airport. I
was awaiting my flight home when the news came that I
would be grounded at the Hartford airport due to fog and
other weather conditions. Before the news arrived, I had been
told the flight was merely delayed. So, to kill time, I took the
airline's free meal pass and ate at the magnificant restaurant
in the terminal. You would think the powers that be could
come up with a better name for an airport building than "ter-

minal" wouldn't you, I mean, with all the airline mishaps and bombings? Anyway, I filled my stomach full with all the delicacies I could purchase with my meal pass.

After gorging myself, and I did feel a little ashamed at the time, I went back to find out when I could board the plane. It was then that the airline told me the news and offered to put me up at the Howard Johnson's hotel. I was taken in an airline bus, along with flight attendants and a pilot or two, to our place of lodging. It was then that my odyssey began. First of all, there was a chef's convention taking place right in the facility where I was staying. I mean to tell you, in a large hall was displayed every kind of delicacy anyone could imagine. It was a culinary dream come true. If I hadn't eaten so much at that dumb airport, I could have sampled exotic goodies all evening. But, alas, I couldn't eat a bite.

As I was waiting to get my room, a famous bowler came up behind me. There had been a big tournament that week in Hartford and this fellow was staying at the same hotel I was. He was my "idol" so far as bowlers go. Having been on a church bowling league, I had often pretended to be this man confidently sliding up to the line and releasing my ball for a perfect 300 game. I had seen him bowl a perfect game on television once. My highest game had only been 228. I even confessed that to him. He laughed and was glad that I was a fan. I got his autograph as we chatted. Funny thing about airports and hotels. It is when in transit that I meet celebrities. Orson Bean dazzled me at LAX once. I gave him a copy of my most recent book. He informed me that he wasn't an atheist, but a theist. I told him that was a start.

Anyway, I was tired and made my way to my room. I didn't even turn on the TV. All I could do was lay down in my bed and fall asleep with my clothes on. I didn't even turn down the covers. It is here that the *nah na nah na nah na nah na* music begins to fade in. Into the wee hours of the morning, maybe 2 or 3 a.m., I got out of bed and went to the bathroom. I remember splashing some water onto my face and wiping it with a hand towel. It awakened me enough to see that I needed to get ready for bed. I took off my clothes and turned down the covers and snuggled into bed for an uninterrupted snooze.

Next morning, I awoke fully dressed and lying on top of the bed that was still made. I had been lying on the bed- spread. At first I thought I had just been dreaming of getting up in the night and getting out of my street clothes. Next, I went into the bathroom to freshen up. Every single towel, and there were three bath towels, three hand towels, three wash- cloths, plus the terrycloth floor mat, was lying flat on the floor one on top of the other, stacked neatly, large towels on the bottom, floor mat on top, then hand towels on top, then washcloths on top of those; all of them were soaking wet. Water was all over the floor. Neither the toilet, nor sink, nor bath tub were leaking. I hadn't even taken a bath. And yet, here I was, standing in the middle of the bathroom, sur- rounded by a deluge. It was the strangest thing to date that has ever happened to me, and that includes a lot of strange things.

I felt foolish telling anyone what had happened. But I did ask one of the hotel maids if anyone could have come into my room with a pass key at night. She asked which room I was in. I told her it was room 66. She smiled and said in broken English. "Oh, dat ist da rum dat ist hunted."

"Hunted?" I asked. "You know," she answered. "Hunted, like wist ghosts ahnd tings."

Nah na nah na nah na nah na nah na nah na . . .

I was speechless. I was in room 66 and on the sixth floor of the hotel. I am sure some numerologist could make a bigger story than I have out of those numbers. I was never one to be superstitious, but I must admit that I had a chilling feeling about what had happened. And the more I thought about it, the more I realized that nobody could have come into the room from the hallway because the room had been deadbolt locked twice with a safety chain to boot. There was no bal- cony and no adjacent room.

To this day I do not know what happened. With some imagination I could talk myself into some alien encounter. I am a believer, of course, in the spiritual realm, but not in ghosts and things that go bump in the night. Or even things that go slosh in the night. Truth is stranger than fiction. I wonder what Rod Serling could have done with this story plot. I surely don't know what to do with it, as you can see. I didn't even shave that morning or brush my teeth. Whether Casper or one of his relatives took a shower in my bathroom that evening, I do not know. But I do know this. I'm glad I didn't eat any more at that chef's convention. Who knows what might have happened then. Please pass the Rolaids.

My Former Habit

For years it had been painfully intrusive in my life. A habit begun as a youngster. Its influence grew on me day by day until it was so ingrained in my routine that I had difficulty admitting I had become addicted. Why it held me captive for so long is a question I may never fully answer. But "held me" it did. And I barely escaped its binding presence in my life.

This ugly demonic intrusion would begin in the early waking hours each day, manifesting itself as a gnawing need that seemed to be overpowering. It called to me. It beckoned me. And I readily gave in, without really giving it any thought. It became so much a part of my routine that it was like brushing my teeth or eating breakfast. It became a necessity. Of course, there was one glaring difference. Brushing and eating were necessary for health reasons. My habit merely distracted me from a more focused existence.

It never once occurred to me that I was addicted until a friend suggested I try to live an entire day without satisfying this overwhelming urge. I tried and failed. I found myself, only hours after my self-imposed abstinence, longing for the comfort of my old familiar desire. Desire! Yes, that was it. The tug at my will went far beyond addiction to compulsive desperation. I had to give in to those urgent impulses or somehow feel disjointed and out of sync.

It has been suggested, time and time again, that the best way for an addict to overcome his behavior is to first admit his dependence. This I did. And that was the turning point in my way out of this addictive bondage. I have been free of the control of this power in my life for more than three years. And I must confess, I rarely miss it. It is amazing how much more work I can get done in a day. I have a great deal more time to smell the roses. Family and friends are now given much of my undivided attention, which is probably the best I have to offer them. I actually find myself enjoying the quietude of reading. The Bible. Religious journals. The extra time I have for writing alone is cathartic. But, most importantly, I feel deep satisfaction in knowing that something so profoundly addictive can be overcome.

Maybe what I have decided for my life isn't for everyone. I certainly have not become a crusader about this. Perhaps some would differ with me. But I do proclaim that giving up television has been good for my spirit. It seemed like every time I turned it on there was invariably a story involving sex, violence, perversion or all three. And it was insidious. For me TV became intellectual poison. Vegetating in front of the sewage that humanistic producers were pandering to the public surely can't be a discerning disciple's cup of tea.

Being a television junkie robbed me of so many hours of life that I am now eager to make up for lost time. I can never reclaim the wasted years. The average family consumes 7.8 hours of TV per day. Without being preachery, if that is possible, I ask my fellow Christians to be candid and ask yourselves: "Am I being a good steward of my time and spiritual health by consuming as much television as I do daily?" It's a tough question to answer truthfully. But it's a start.

Good luck.

The Church of Hypocrisy

My wife and I were driving through the plains of Texas, heading toward one of our favorite college lectureships. The sun was shining in spite of the wind and chilly February temperatures. Since it was about the typical time for morning church services, we located a congregation in a town that looked to be about 20,000 in population. We arrived just after Bible classes were dismissed. This gave us about fifteen minutes to mingle, and hopefully, visit with some of the members before worship.

We were immediately impressed with how large the auditorium was. It must have been large enough to seat at least 1,500 people. We even commented on how refreshing it was to see such a large church in a moderately small town. Alas, our judgment was premature. A few nodded their heads at us as we stood inside the building. Feeling somewhat uncomfortable at not being greeted by anyone, we seated ourselves. Within ten minutes about 250 were in the auditorium when the service began.

Though we are surely not judges of individuals nor entire churches, after leaving this assembly we concluded between ourselves that we had visited a church that was in the throes of death. It held glimpses of former greatness, but was a pale shadow of its prior self. After worship, the preacher stood at one of the many exits. We left through "his" door in hopes that at least the parson would speak to us. To our chagrin, as he shook out the flock, he shook us out as well. I could almost feel the tug of his handshake as he pulled me along with his hypocritical "Good to see ya'" and no eye contact. "Next!"

I suspect there are a myriad of churches not unlike this one. Churches that have lost their first love. Churches that have forgotten their commission. Churches that have simply grown old and are ready to have a funeral but nobody's told them yet. And there are countless reasons why churches end up this way, and all of the reasons do not have to do with demographics. Allow me to share a few scenarios that I am

personally aware of that have caused churches to lose their
positive influence in their communities.

A widowed mother, with five children under the ages of
15, faithfully attended church services. She had a low paying
job and struggled to keep food on the table. Unable to purchase a car, she had to walk several miles to the church building. During the four years she was a member of this congregation, not once did anyone offer to give her and the children
a ride, in rain or snow. Not once did anyone have the family
over for a meal. Not once was this dear sister offered any
assistance with her children or finances. And, of course, the
woman never asked. She just left that church. A couple of her
children dropped out entirely. Do we wonder why?

A mother and her two daughters began attending church
services at a congregation near their home. The girls became
active in the youth programs. The mother not only attended
most of the services, but after a few weeks, had formally
placed her membership. Other members were friendly and
made all of the typical social comments that one would expect
before and after church services. Six months later the mother
had a medical crisis and wasn't able to be at services. Since
she had not become close to any particular person, she failed
to call the church office and tell anyone why she was unable
to be there. No one seemed to notice her absence, nor the
absence of her two girls. She received not a call, not a card,
not one inquiry. She moved her membership. Do we wonder
why?

A church hired a "new" evangelist. Their reason for dis-
missing their four previous preachers within a period of six
years was that they were not evangelistic enough. So this new
parson was given the impression that the church wanted to be
on the cutting edge of evangelism and needed someone with
the will and the enthusiasm to inspire the church in that
regard. After several weeks of lessons and sermons outlining
the proposed outreach ministry to the community, when it
came time for the program to begin, only two members of the
500 member congregation showed up to help, and only one of
the eight elders was a part of that number. The evangelist

became disheartened and shortly afterward began the search for another congregation. Do we wonder why?

A visitor who had just moved to town, beginning a new job, attempting to start afresh after years of struggle, arrived at the church house eager to meet Christians and become part of a warm congregation once again. He did not know the exact times of the services so entered the auditorium while an adult class was in progress. Several class members turned and stared. No one offered to give him a clue as to where the class was in the text. After class was dismissed, and before the worship hour, nobody spoke to the gentleman. He was not wearing a suit, but he certainly was not dressed like a possible transient, though that shouldn't have made a difference. He noticed this aloofness but tried to persuade himself that he might be imagining things, or that people might be shy. So he sat through the worship hour looking forward to meeting people after dismissal. Again, he was ignored. Not an invitation to lunch. Not any interest in where he was from or what his name was. He didn't return. Do we wonder why?

A congregation had over $100,000 in a savings account. A visiting missionary asked for permission to speak to the church leaders about his work. He needed an additional $100 a month to complete his support. The church declined, for whatever reasons. There was no mission involvement by this church listed on their financial statements. Yet, one month later the church was led in pledging over $500,000 to build a gymnasium on their property, a facility they euphemistically would call a "family life center." Do we wonder why the world remains lost?

Other scenarios could be offered, but these are ones made known to me that help make my point. It seems that many churches are so at ease in Zion and so accustomed to business as usual that they have evolved into mere guardians of the status quo. Of such a church, Jesus said that it made Him sick to His stomach. Leaders need to keep checking the vital signs of their congregations. Some churches need immediate resuscitation. Others, spiritual cadavers, need to be put to rest. Do we wonder why?

Lady Barbara?

Why she liked to be called "Lady" I still do not know. I understand she was from the south and that it was quite proper to display such an ornament before one's name. I don't think it was intended to signify nobility. And I know for a fact it wasn't in reference to this woman's behavior, for a "lady" she wasn't. A woman, perhaps. But definitely not a lady. Yet, she had trained everyone to call her "Lady Barbara."

I first met her while conducting a gospel meeting at a congregation for which I was later invited to minister. I had approached the church house door before she had and, being the gentleman that I am, held the door open for her. She stopped in her tracks and refused to enter the building. I continued to hold the door open until it occurred to me that she was making some sort of statement about independence or something of the sort. Just as I was about to give up and go inside, she barked, "If I had wanted you to hold the door open for me, I would have asked you to!" I smiled and went on inside. That was my unforgettable introduction to sister Barbara. She never got a second chance to make a first impression with me, and the impression she had made was reaffirmed time and time again.

During the meeting, after each session, I would stand by the main exit and greet people as they departed. Most folk were kind enough to say some little comment about the lesson. "Fine sermon, brother Goad," was the usual. "Best lesson I have ever heard on that subject," was rare. "I sure do appreciate how clearly you explain the Bible," was one of my favorites. But one comment I recall wasn't said directly to my face. It was made by Lady Barbara, to another member in the foyer, for all to hear: "I don't know when I've heard less Bible and more opinion in my life." I got the message. Ouch!

A parson only needs one member like that to make life on the planet almost miserable. I should have read the handwriting on the wall and refused to move to this wonderful fellowship when asked to minister there a few years later. Perhaps I had hoped someone might have straightened out this vicious woman by then. Or maybe I was thinking she might have moved on to another church, seeking out other opportunities to do what she did best. But when I arrived, there she was, part of the welcoming committee. She had brought an elaborately decorated cake to the house, letting me know she had done the art work herself. It was beautiful. She put it on the table with these words: "No need to send me a thank you card. None of the other preachers ever did." Aha! I was in for more. As she left the parsonage with another lady from church, I heard her say, "He'll be lucky to last a year." Did she know something I didn't?

Lady Barbara was quite an attractive woman. She was past middle age but had hair as dark as a young woman's. And it didn't look dyed. I'm sure it was natural. Had she not possessed the spirit of ugliness, she could have been a beautiful woman. I mean, on the outside she had all the attributes. But the meanness on the inside, that escaped all too frequently, diminished her in the eyes of the many she chose to offend. I found myself praying for her.

A few years into working with that congregation of which she was a member, we invited a friend of mine to come for a revival meeting. He was good. I knew it. That's why I encouraged the elders to have him come and be with us. His lessons were as I had expected, excellent. The last evening of the meeting, as my friend and I were "shaking the brethren out of the church house," along came Lady Barbara, lips pursed and eyes flashing, ready for one of her barbs. I had already warned my preacher friend to beware, but little did I know I would again be the brunt of her observation.

"Well, Brother Jones," she said loudly to my friend, "I haven't heard good preaching like that in at least two years."

Yep. That's right. I had been with the congregation exactly two years.

Throughout my ministry I have prided myself on not having some hobbyhorse to ride from the pulpit. By hobbyhorse, I mean some pet subject that I might bring up in any given sermon, regardless of what the sermon was actually about. If I had a hobbyhorse, I suppose it was soul winning or unity or something like that. But with Lady Barbara, I was tempted to develop a hobby real fast. I wanted so often to preach on the sins of the tongue. I did a few times. I so much wanted to deliver homilies on gentleness and kindness, and did as often as possible without being obvious. But our critical sister in Christ didn't get the message.

After a few years of ministry at this congregation I decided that Lady Barbara was my thorn in the flesh. I had prayed thrice to have it removed, but God let me know His grace was sufficient. So I accepted her ladyship, warts and all, as one who didn't know any better and never would. I tried not to be defensive. I tried not to get my feelings hurt. My hide got thicker. Her slings and arrows got sharper and more frequent. I hunkered down for the long haul. But she was wearing combat boots.

One Wednesday evening sister Barbara approached me after Bible class and said, "Brother Goad, I don't like the approach you are using for evangelism." We had been using marked Bibles to get a prospect's attention. As we handed out these Bibles, we would ask for a home Bible study. I wasn't all that excited about the method myself. But it was working. We had witnessed 68 baptisms in 8 months. I had tried to get the membership to see that "friendship evangelism" is what would work best, but for some of the members, who weren't very friendly in the first place, they didn't seem to catch the vision. So, here I was, teaching people how to reach out to the lost by way of one method that seemed to be successful at that time and place.

There I stood. I could be kind and smile a hypocritical smile to cover up how I really felt inside, or I could blow up and let her see that she had gotten to me with her caustic criticisms. Or, better still, I could be wise as a serpent and harmless as a dove and do what my judo instructor had taught me. "Use their energy against them, Steve."

So, I pretended not to hear her and said, "I beg your pardon?" I was hoping she would come to her senses and realize what she was doing. But alas, she fired away once again.

"I said I don't like the approach you are using in reaching out to the lost of the community."

I looked her square in the face and replied, "Oh, you don't? Then please tell me what method *you* are using that has been successful for you."

Total silence. You could have heard a pin drop. It was deafening. She just stood there and glared at me. Her face became flushed. Then, she turned on her heels and left in a huff, never speaking to me again, or ever looking me in the eye. From that day on, in classes and during sermons, she would protest my presence by holding her head down. It was sort of like boycotting my teaching. She may have been reading her Bible or filing her fingernails for all I know. As much as I was tempted to do so, I never got the satisfaction of questioning her behavior and calling her to repent. Perhaps I failed her in my silence, because a woman like that surely needed someone to force accountability on her for her evil ways.

It was a fortunate set of circmstances for me that she had approached me that evening. For, had she not, I would have been the brunt of her continued harangues until I could take it no more. Later that evening, I recalled the various other times when she displayed the opposite spirit that Christ asked of us all. I remembered the time she had come to me on a Sunday morning and screeched, "I don't like that sort of thing." She was pointing to a lapel pin I was wearing that said, "Jesus First." She explained that it was pretentious and hypocritical to wear such showy signs of discipleship, sort of like the Pharisee Jesus talked about who said that sanctimonious prayer. The very next Sunday, she was wearing an Eastern Star pin on her blouse. I went up to her (yes, I know, this was mean spirited of me, but I just couldn't resist the opportunity) and pointed to her sorority pin and said, "I don't like that sort of thing." She missed the point entirely. I never saw her wear that pin again.

I recalled the many occasions when she would come to me to correct some grammatical mistakes I had made in my lessons. And she was always the first to tell me if there was a typo in the church bulletin I edited. She would often suggest sermons be shortened. (She never once suggested they be lengthened.) On one occasion, before the Lord's Supper, I read a poignant selection from Jim Bishop's book, *The Day Christ*

Died. Afterward, she was hot on my heels to inform me that I had quoted from the writing of a Catholic author.

"How dare you quote from profane writings and uninspired authors!" she rebuked.

I asked her, "Lady Barbara, do you sing the songs in our song book?" She was smart. She knew I was setting her up. But I caught her off guard.

"Yes!" she hissed, "why do you ask?"

I explained, "Do you think Fanny Crosby and John Wesley and Martin Luther and L.O. Sanderson and Tillet S. Tedlie are inspired authors? Yet you sing their prose and poetry out loud, right here in front of God and everyone else."

I also went on to point out that even the apostle Paul quoted from uninspired poets. Again, I had called her bluff, but with no satisfaction. For she, as she always did under such indictment, turned and walked silently away, shaking her head in disgust.

One thing for which I must give Lady Barbara credit: she was a prophetess. Yesiree! For one day she predicted the departure of parson Goad. I had just offered the invitation. It was my lot to offer a short invitation on Wednesday evenings after all the classes had finished their Bible studies. This particular Wednesday evening, I had made an extra strong appeal because we had several young people who were ready to obey the gospel, and we also had a couple that we had been studying with that were on the verge of making a decision. So I pled more strongly than usual. I made it clear that without Christ and His atoning blood, we were all lost. As was typical, Lady Barbara didn't like what I had said, nor the way I had said it.

She came to me spitting mad and said, "Goad, I'm sick and tired of you judging everyone in this church." It was the first time she had called me "Goad." She usually was "polite" and "charming" and called me "Brother Goad." And I didn't have an inkling of what she was talking about.

I pled ignorance. "I'm sorry, Barbara, but I have no idea what you mean."

(Yes, I had called her "Barbara" instead of my usual "Lady Barbara" or "sister Barbara." Maybe I was inadvertantly responding to her rudeness at calling me "Goad." Or maybe I was sending her a signal that I didn't think she was a lady. Not by a long shot!)

She explained, "You get awfully high and mighty when giving the invitation. You ought to be more humble."

Yes, I admit it. I lost my cool. I had read where we were to be slow to anger. Well, I figured the several years that I had had to put up with Lady Barbara had accredited me enough points to let her have it just once. It dawned on me that her name was appropriate. Barbara. Like in Barb! Every word was a barb. She was like barbed wire, ready to draw blood at the slightest provocation.

I squared my shoulders and looked into her fuming face and said, "Barbara, if you don't like my ministry style, why don't you just go some place where you can be happy?"

This is when she prophesied.

She snapped, "Listen, Goad, I've seen preachers come and go from this place. I've been here a lot longer than you have. And I'll be here when you are long gone."

And she was right. A few months later a wonderful church asked me to work with them, and I used sister Barbara as my excuse for leaving. Oh, I never told anyone she was my excuse. I mean, in my own head I didn't really want to leave that good church. (It had to have been a good church to tolerate the likes of Lady Barbara.) So I used the barbacious Lady Barbara as my inalienable right to relocate to a better climate.

I don't hate the woman. I have pity for her. I hear she has mellowed somewhat in her old age. Sometimes people get mean when they get old. I guess Barbara was born mean and is growing sweet in her senior years. I hope so. I have prayed for her often. She wrote me a letter a few years ago. It was short and terse. It was the closest thing to an apology she could muster. I think her conscience had gotten the best of her and she seemed to be attempting to right some old wrongs she had been guilty of. Perhaps that is why the note was so short. I mean, just think of all the people she must have had to write to.

The note simply said, "I hope you are doing well in your ministry. I miss hearing you say, 'Good morning, church!' I'm praying for you."

Was it an apology? Well, it was close enough for me.

Vestibule Remembrances

"A word aptly spoken is like apples of gold in settings of silver"
(Proverbs 25:11).

This recollection is meant neither to be an exercise in bragging nor complaining. It is an attempt to reveal some of the depths and heights of human nature, to show how even Christians are able to speak without hesitation and utter things intended to sting rather than heal. Why it seems to be perpetual "open season" on preachers, I don't quite fully understand, but I suppose those who frequent the pews must assume ministers of the word have tough hides.

Over some almost 30 years of having the privilege of standing in the pulpit proclaiming the stories of the Bible and the message of salvation, I have been the recipient of kind words far beyond my deserving, as well as cutting words that no honest heart should have to endure, especially from those fellow disciples who are to hold up the hands of the evangelist rather than undermine his message and quench his spirit. But, alas, I share with you some of the words uttered in passing in the church foyer after the sermon of the hour had been delivered.

As mentioned previously, one sister, who had been my nemesis from the day I had arrived in town, uttered these words of encouragement to a visiting preacher: "Brother Jones, that was the best sermon I have heard in at least two years." Yes, I had been with the congregation exactly two years.

A deacon took me to task for using an illustration about a construction boss, a parable if you will, whereby I inserted one of our members into the story. The deacon got my attention in the foyer by shouting, "Brother Goad, you are a blatant liar!" He went on to chide me for personalizing an illustration. I think he was sore that I hadn't used him in the parable.

Most folk are precious in their encouragement. I have had far more "Best sermon I've ever heard's" than I deserve. Some have simply said, "You make me think." This, to me, is one of the greatest compliments of all for a parson. When someone compares me to a faithful and beloved fellow preacher of renown, I am always taken aback. "You remind me so much of Jimmy Allen." It's hard not to have a swelled head under such flattery. Once in a while someone will say, "You spoke right to my heart, and I'm going to do something about it."

Occasionally people will assume things not so, and make comments accordingly. "You never speak on marriage and divorce," someone once said. "Are you afraid of the subject?" This infrequent attender hadn't noticed, for obvious reasons, that I had had several lessons on the subject, as well as Bible class discussion on it. If I had said something as insulting, such as, "You never seem to be at the assemblies and classes. Are you afraid of getting too religious?", they would have had their feelings hurt and no telling what they would have said to the elders about the rude and heartless preacher.

Joe Barnett and I are both sensitive to those who love to give "organ recitals" in the foyer. These are the folks who can't keep their surgeries to themselves. So, if you ask a casual, "How are you?" you might as well get ready for several minutes of captivity to medical procedures. "No thanks! I really don't need to see the scars."

One fellow, who let me know early on that he was not a fan club member of mine, told me after a sermon on commitment and lukewarmness, "You can catch more flies with honey than with vinegar." He actually said "bees," but I knew what he meant. Of course, I didn't have the time to tell him I wasn't in the fly (or bee) catching business. I did ask him, "Do you love me?" His response was telling: "I'm working on it."

A couple of widow ladies, whom I adored and still do, came to me in tandem one Sunday and said, "Brother Goad, why don't you preach the 'old time gospel' instead of all this modern stuff?" When I further questioned them about what they meant, they wanted me to tack on the plan of salvation to any sermon I offered. Who knows; maybe that's a good idea. We never know who's present.

An elder in the church took it upon himself to tell me one day, "Steve, why not cut the sermons shorter. A lot of people think they're too long." It sounded like he took a poll, but I doubt it. Funny thing, I have never had an eldership, a deaconship, a widowship, or a teenship ever come and say, "Brother Goad, we love the word so much! Could you do us a favor and preach longer sermons?"

Chapter Six

Journeys to Eternity

In His Memory

All of us have memorable characters that come and go in our lives as we matriculate to adulthood. He was just such a character. Like a Damon Runyon figure, Timothy Hickey will always be alive so long as I have his memory in my heart.

Timmy was the only kid smaller than I in our class in grade school. Perhaps that is why I enjoyed his friendship so much. Around Timmy I looked bigger. His hair was never combed and the cleanliness of his hands was doubtful. He was from the other side of the tracks, though we didn't talk about that kind of thing so much in my era, or at least in my neck of the woods, which as I recall wasn't that far from the tracks either. Timmy lived in "Dogpatch." Why that part of our neighborhood was named after Li'l Abner's environs I do not know. But it wasn't the cleanest nor safest place in the world to be. Sort of a war zone for the uninvited.

Part of my paper route was in the middle of Dogpatch. One day some jerks who were older and bigger than I tried to give me some trouble. They started taking my folded papers and throwing them back and forth. They tipped my bicycle over on its side. They more or less harassed me until I was about to cry. Then Timmy walked up. I didn't know he was such a scrapper until that day. In spite of his small stature, he had a wiriness about him and hints of muscles that apparently the neighborhood thugs had already had personal experience with. It was a good thing I had befriended him in school because I discovered that day he could have whipped me with one hand tied behind his back.

Timmy walked up to those boys who were several years our senior and said something on the order of this, as best as I can recall: "Hey, guys, I'll make a bet with you. I'll bet Stevie and I can whip all five of you." They looked like they had been hit with a stun gun. "Why go startin' somethin' with us?" one of them asked Timmy. "Well, it looks like you been startin' somethin' with my friend, Stevie," he explained. "And I'm here to finish it." It was then I learned the influence little Timmy wielded in Dogpatch. Like the men who were ready to stone the woman caught in the very act, all five hoodlums began to leave one at a time with their heads down low.

From that day on, Timothy Hickey and I became even closer pals. He never was my best friend, but he was one of those friends you could count on whenever you needed him. He knew he could depend on me to help him with his math homework. I knew he would provide safe passage through Dogpatch, whether I was on my paper route, or just in the neighborhood. At school poor Timmy could also count on me for a bologna sandwich and one of my Twinkies. Mostly, Timmy had to eat mashed potato sandwiches or jelly and peanut butter sandwiches. When I gave little Timmy one of my fried chicken legs one day, you'd have thought I'd given him a million dollars from the look on his face.

In high school Timmy and I began drifting apart. He was

such a tough little guy that he excelled in wrestling. I tried wrestling but didn't enjoy being in such close proximity to sweaty boys who didn't wear much deodorant. Choir and stage productions were more my forte. So we didn't find our-selves in each others' presence much. But when we passed in the hallway we always gave each other a knowing smile.

Vietnam found Timmy called up early in the conflict. He didn't last two weeks on the front lines. When I got the news, I cried like a baby. Tears swell up in my eyes now as I remem-ber his friendship. Why he had to go fight people he didn't know to defend something he didn't understand is beyond me. But he went anyway. And if there ever was a soldier who gave it his all, I am sure it was Timmy. He died trying to rescue some of his fallen comrades. It was the same spirit that res-cued me from the tough guys in Dogpatch. The medals he won posthumously are reminders to his family that he was a man of valor. But I will always remember him as a friend who was eager to be kind to those in need. He always seemed to care more for others than for himself.

Timmy never looked for a fight. I'm thankful I hadn't been stupid enough to test his mettle simply because of his small stature. But Timmy never ran from a fight, either. And as much as he may have wanted to, he didn't run from Vietnam. Thanks for remembering Timmy with me and the 58,000 oth-ers who gave their lives for freedom in that horrible war nobody won.

God's Elder

Why do I love elders so much? It is a puzzling question, since some elders have caused me more grief than anyone deserves in a lifetime. But they are only human beings with feet of clay just like the rest of us. And I haven't quit liking people, generally, simply because some of them have done me dirty.

From among elders have come some of my closest and dearest friends. When I am sick I call upon the elders to pray for me. When I need counsel, they are there to lend understanding hearts and helpful direction. Certainly many more elders have done good for me than the few who have done me wrong. God's elders are like preachers in that regard. There are good preachers who deserve all the support they receive, and more. Then there are some pathetic men who see the pulpit as a means to an audience and who accept paychecks as hirelings, rather than as rescuers of souls. Thus, I unashamedly confess that I adore the shepherds of God's flock who minister to souls as "men who will give an account."

I am thinking to tell you now of one of my special elders. He was, in many ways, a self-made man. He grew up in poverty. Sometimes it appeared as though the deck were stacked against him. For example, amazingly, the day he graduated from high school his father was arrested for rape. It was on the front page of the local paper. He worked his way through college while raising a family. Some days he had but one or two hours sleep after studying before it was time to go to the job again.

His name was Howard. Of course, this isn't really his name, but I give you a name to make him more personable. Howard loved the church. He especially liked to be close to the men who ministered in the word. He made immediate and deliberate efforts to ingratiate himself with me. And I noticed.

Howard loved his family and delighted in his vocation. His company was indebted to him in many ways. He was a nuts and bolts kind of employee who got the job done, one way or the other. He took to the task of shepherding God's flock with the same enthusiasm. The man loved to tell silly jokes and then laugh at them himself, even if no one else did. A person inclined to quick and superficial judgments might think Howard a dim-witted clown. But that would be a big mistake.

My beloved elder would have tears in his eyes as he finished praying for missionaries and lost souls. He took time to be holy. He was a case study in tolerance and good will. If all of God's presbyters were on par with Howard, the body of Christ would be a whole lot better off.

Howard had an ancestor in the early church: Eutychus. It was Howard who snored during my sermons. He often snored during the singing of the invitation hymn. He suffered from a malady called narcolepsy. It caused him to fall asleep at the most inopportune times. He would fall asleep at board meetings. He would start snoozing during elders' meetings. But he seemed most comfortable under the spell of my lectures.

Dear Howard was a hands-on elder. He sat on the front pew during the worship assembly so that he could assist me in receiving those who responded to the Lord's invitation. He would help me, that is, if he could arise from his slumber. One day I was waxing eloquent, and the louder I got the louder the ZZZZZZ's got emanating from Howard's nasal passages. The decibel level was amazing. It sounded, at times, like a 747 jumbo jet was flying inside the auditorium. In order to capture Howard's immediate attention, at an appropriate point in my lesson I slapped the pulpit with a mighty smack. It startled Howard so much that he literally fell out onto the floor. I wanted to rush down, as Paul must have done for poor old Eutychus, and embrace Howard and lift him up. But he was just too heavy and I knew that he was probably all right. Besides, I didn't want to embarrass him any more than he already was.

What a sweet brother in Christ. He's gone on to eternity and will probably never again fall asleep in church. He ain't a gonna study snore no more. He was ashamed of his affliction.

Actually it was a condition, but he thought of it as an affliction. Strangely, he never fell asleep at the wheel of his car.

I once took it personally when folk slept during my ser-
monizing. Then I decided that if I couldn't keep them awake,
I'd rather have them sleep in the church house than stay
home and nap. I heard of an amazing statistic the other day.
Did you realize that if all Christians on any given Sunday were
laid out end to end, head to head, on church pews, they'd be
a whole lot more comfortable? Gotcha, didn't I? Now I realize
that a lot of us, when we get older, develop conditions that
require medications that occasionally make us groggy. So
every time I see a sleeping Christian in an assembly, I smile
and try to think the best and have the thought of Howard in
the back of my mind. My precious friend and elder in God's
house may have slept from time to time against his wishes,
but I affirm that the man was as industrious as any I've met in
the kingdom.

Sleep on, dear Howard.

Eddie

He was among the first to welcome me to the deep south. I had been invited to minister with a church which, in many ways, showed signs of strength, and whose leadership had said they wanted to grow. Being evangelistic of mind and desiring to be part of a thriving and growing congregation, I accepted their invitation. Eddie was a deacon at this good church. He and I hit if off at once since he, too, cared for the lost of his community. He became my visitation buddy. And we grew to love each other deeply.

Eddie was Lebanese. His last name was Nassar. Having attended one of our Christian colleges, he had tried full-time ministry with a few congregations and still preached occasionally by appointment. But he had decided to take up the business he had learned from his father. Eddie owned and operated a pawn shop. Though his business took up much of his time, he was a wonderful father to his two daughters, and he and his wife were the perfect picture of what a Christian family should be.

Brother Nassar and I would go out on week nights and call on those people who had visited our congregation for the first time. We set up Bible studies and eagerly taught those who were interested in learning about Jesus. We fed on each other's enthusiasm. And we were a good team. I remember one chilly winter evening when we were out, it started to snow. It rarely snowed in that neck of the woods, so Eddie accused me of ordering the snow so I would feel at home, having come from Yankee country and all. We had a good laugh over that. In just a few months we had witnessed 68 souls baptized into Christ. And Eddie was as thrilled as I was for these new members of the body of Christ. One other thing I admired about Eddie, he took new converts under his wing and discipled them. He didn't just let them drift into the church and then drift out the back door a few weeks later, as is often the case. We were one at heart in our willingness to do what had to be done to grow God's family.

It was a day not unlike any other. Eddie had kissed his wife, Harriet, goodbye, and hugged his little girls before leaving for work. I dropped by his store that day to ask him if he was able to teach a lesson in our "new converts" class. He happily agreed. That afternoon, Harriet dropped off his girls, ages 5 and 7, while she made the bank deposit for their business. While she was at the bank, two ruthless hoodlums, that we later learned had been on a cross-country crime spree, came into Eddie's pawn shop to rob him. As his little girls watched in horror, one of the men shot dear brother Eddie in the back as he was turning around to get the money they were demanding.

The next few days found not only Eddie's family, but the entire church family, in total shock and disbelief. Never before had such evil struck so close to home. Surgeons worked feverishly to save him. Dr. Bob Green, another deacon of the church, was there to keep us posted on how the surgery was going. But, alas, the bullet had traveled up Eddie's spine and into his heart, doing fatal damage. We all wept tears of disbelief in the waiting room when Bob brought the tragic news.

The funeral was the hardest I had ever had to conduct. Our gospel quartet, of which I was a tenor, sang for the occasion. It was all I could do to keep my composure. Never before had I made such a close connection with someone in such a short span of time, only to have it so suddenly interrupted. It was like losing the brother I never had. The huge crowd that came for his memorial service was testimony to the affection and high esteem held for Eddie by so many. I felt so sad for Harriet and the girls. It was such a tragedy for these girls to have one day had a father and husband, and the next day to be orphaned and widowed. Life, even for the elect of God, is a struggle at best. Eddie's struggle was over, prematurely so. And all that was left was his sweet memory and his legacy of love which remained. And we all tried to make some sense of it.

How do we handle this kind of deep and personal grief? Not very well, I confess. I was so angry at those men; I suspect I would have taken a gun and shot them dead had I been given the opportunity. So many of us were asking the same question: "Why us, Lord?" After years of litigation, the men were executed. But it was a bittersweet revenge for the family. A father's son was still gone. A wife's mate was no longer there to comfort and hold at night. And my brother in Christ could no longer make me laugh at some idiotic point I had made in a Bible study.

I've never written about Eddie's passing until now, except for the expression of sympathy in the church bulletin at the time. I don't know why I felt compelled to share it with you now in this forum. Maybe it's just to keep his memory alive. But perhaps, more importantly, it is a reminder that life is so very fragile and we do not have any guarantee that there will be any tomorrows. Inequitably, it seems to most of us, it does indeed rain on the just and the unjust. May we allow Eddie's tragedy to be a reminder that we are temporarily occupying probation time on this planet. And when we are ready to pass over to the other side, or when we are struggling with all our might to keep from letting go of the here and now, may we find ourselves engaged in the business of doing His will and being His children.

Hear me now. Kiss your mate. Tell him/her and your parents and children you love them. Embrace your children and look into their eyes and let them feel the strength of your presence. Take time to be holy. It's trite, I know, but Eddie helps remind me to live each day with gratitude and thanksgiving for the things in life that genuinely matter. Family. Friends. Salvation. Hope. Eternity.

Thanks, Eddie.

Slings & Arrows

He was my first introduction to what a minister of the word ought to be. Not that I hadn't heard other so-called "gospel preachers" in the past. I had. But I had previously been of such tender ages that my concentration on what was emanating from the pulpit was, well, simply lacking. I was more interested in drawing crayola pictures and observing the funny looking hats the women wore to church. I especially had lots of fun playing with those funeral fans with the picture of the Last Supper on one side. They had been donated to the church in hopes we would remember the advertised funeral parlor when one of our members came to dispatching time. The preachers who came before Brother Bobo might have been powerful in the Scriptures and mighty in oratorical skills, but I was too busy sleeping, asking mom to tickle my back or making faces at other kids to pay much attention.

It is amazing how unfocused kids are. I mean, when I was a kid, my mind was on several items all at the same time, it seemed.

Sunday was an extremely special day for the Goad family. I can't remember not being at a church house on Sundays from my earliest recollections. A Brother Peck is the first preacher's name I can recall from my early years. He was loved by all, or at least I thought so at the time. I loved him. He always patted my head and called me by name. Most adults didn't take time to learn the name of a kid. Why wouldn't anyone want to love a parson? But then, that's my story, isn't it?

Even though I don't remember one single lesson from my early years in the church house, and by lesson I mean a homily or sermon actually presented from the pulpit, I do remember one glaring impression from all those times we were in those assemblies as a family: Church was important! Nothing short of a calamity could keep us from being at the appointed place during the designated hours. And all down through the years I have never been able to shake the notion that being together as a church family is important, even essential. Church is a part of what I am. And now that I have learned why the body of Christ is so important, it affirms the devotion that my parents had for being children of God.

Childhood memories of "church" are still with me. I liked the aromas of the occasion. Sunday reminded me of the peppermint gum fragrance that emanated from Mom's purse and the congregate smell of the gathered crowd with all those various perfumes and colognes intermingling. Some might even say it was an odor. But it always seemed to be the same. Someone could have blindfolded me and taken me into that church house and I would have known where I was by the smell of all those scented saints. Another fragrance that delighted my olfactory senses was the wafting essence of the fruit of the vine as it was passed before me. All of that, and more, had reminded me of how much "Jesus loves me, this I know."

It was out of this background and this beloved history that I finally began to take notice of what was being said from behind that wooden box on the raised platform in the direction toward where all of those pews were facing. And when I took notice, the one speaking behind that box was David Bobo. Actually he was Dr. David Bobo. I must have been nine or ten when I started taking notice of what Brother Bobo was saying. We all called him "Brother" Bobo. I called all adults brother or sister so and so. It was polite. It showed respect. It was a nice tradition. I miss it today. But Brother Bobo was getting inside little Stevie Goad's head with the words he delivered so eloquently.

I didn't know Brother Bobo was a doctor. He never wore a white jacket. He never carried a stethoscope. He didn't flaunt his education. He had amassed several scholastic degrees, two of which were doctorates in Biblical languages. He was one of the two most educated parsons in our fellowship, next to Earl West who was already well known for his tomes on Restoration History. But, one thing I recall about Brother Bobo was his humility. He would not have wanted someone to elevate him above anyone else simply because he was highly educated. He didn't relish in titles. Yet others, mostly preachers in the area, seemed to be intimidated by his scholarship. At least, that is my assessment from my vantage point as I write today. Then, one might observe that I was coming of age. I was stepping, or maybe it was more like leaping, into that nebulous period in one's life we referred to as "the age of accountability." I was listening to the lessons. I was being reminded of my sins. I was being discipled and made ready for rebirth.

This story is really about David Bobo and not about my conversion experience. Although Brother Bobo eventually did baptize me, the greatest thing he did for me was to tell me the old, old story of Jesus over and over again in as many ways as possible until my youthful mind could grasp the awesomeness of it. And even with his PhD's he was able to deliver the messages at a level even this Hoosier lad could understand. Little did I know, however, that this dear minister was ahead of his time in the area of tolerance. Because of this, he was accused of compromise during much of his lifetime. He was really guilty of practicing the kind of, "if they are not against us they are for us," tolerance that we are now seeing practiced all around us today. He taught in a school some brethren thought was "suspect": Christian Theological Seminary at Butler University in Indianapolis, Indiana.

David Bobo was a lover of souls and a man eager to see those souls obey the gospel of Christ. He loved all of his brothers and sisters and did not spend his ministry attempting to identify who they all were. He did not practice pronouncing shibboleth in the proper manner. Such matters seemed of little concern to him. He accepted any practicing disciple who had been baptized into Christ, as a family member and equal. And he took a lot of abuse for his tolerance. The strange part of this story is where the abuse originated. It came from his own fellowship.

Brother Bobo gave a prophetic lecture at one of our Christian colleges. Because of this lone lecture, he was summarily drawn and quartered by the gnat strainers of his day. He was "written up" in the party papers and ecclesiastical slander sheets. He was marked as a false teacher. He was cas-

tigated from Dan to Beersheba for suggesting what N.B.
Hardeman had said a generation earlier, and what had been
said even before then: "We may not be the only Christians,
but we are Christians only." I don't know if he ever got an
invitation to speak at one of "our" lectureships again. He
ended up spending his long ministry in Indianapolis with
lesser men than he snapping at his holy heels, trying to prove
what a heretic and blasphemer he was.

Some years later, a gathering of area preachers called
brother Bobo on the carpet for some infraction. I think it was
in response to a bulletin article he had written on unity or tolerance (or some other such harebrained topic). A meeting of
the powers that be was initiated and they all gathered to give
the liberal minister a "fair" hearing. I wasn't present at that
meeting, but I recall my father-in-law describing it as a sham
and a disgrace. He admitted that he was ashamed to have
even been present. As I recall, it was said that the most gentlemanly and Christlike person in attendance was the one
being crucified at the hands of narrow-minded, modern-day
Pharisees. The area preachers had intended to make an example of Brother Bobo in a misguided attempt to stem the tide of
the ever present enemy, namely liberalism, that was, they
claimed, malignantly encroaching upon the church. They had
challenged him on his position of not judging as sinners and
erring brethren those who sang with the accompaniment of
instruments.

In my years of ministering in the word of God, I have
received my share of pronouncements against me. I have been
"writ' up" in not a few party organs and have had anathemas
leveled against me. But never have I had to endure the unrelenting persecution that my dear mentor and friend suffered
almost daily. And he suffered from his own. We can understand when the world attacks us. But it is a sad and disgraceful
commentary on Christian unity when we attack and devour
one another in the name of keeping the church pure and con-
tending for the faith. It's not how Paul dealt with Peter's waf-
fling on Judaism. It's not how Jesus dealt with outright sin in
the lives of those He rescued.

This story of one personable parson is testimony to all of those who have suffered the slings and arrows of little men, spiteful men who out of jealously or bitterness or self-promotion have tried to stifle and undermine the ministries of those they judged wrongly. Several years into my full time ministry, Brother Bobo called me on the phone. Acting in the capacity of an elder of my old home church, he asked me to come and conduct a gospel meeting for them. I was thrilled that this wonderful man would allow a boy who grew up under his tutelage to come back home and speak to the church. After all, a prophet is without honor in his own home and among his own people.

When I shared the news of my invitation, several concerned people, colleagues and friends, warned me that it would not be good for my reputation to hold a meeting where the infamous brother David Bobo was minister. No, indeed. I was told that if I cared for future invitations for meetings and lectureships elsewhere that I had better decline the invitation. Shamefully, I took some of that advice. I told my dear brother that I could not come because of the controversy surrounding his ministry and the church for which he labored. He understood and never held it against me. This I know, for a year or so later I came to my senses and called him and asked if I could come and have a meeting there. After all, I would speak at St. Peter's Cathedral if someone gave me an invitation. The elders there didn't put a muzzle on me or tell me what to preach. It was an open pulpit and all the direction they gave me was that they wished me to speak from the word of God in Christian love.

The meeting was a marvelous experience for me, as I recall. It was a warm reunion with many old friends, and a few former enemies. I was allowed to peddle my wares, a book I had just had published by Standard Publishing entitled *Kicking Against the Goads*. It was at that meeting that I told Brother Bobo that his preaching was the first that had ever reached my youthful mind with the gospel message. And to be able to share the Word in return with the man who first captured my tender awareness with the reality of eternity and accountability, was a singular privilege I would not soon forget.

Pray for preachers and ministers and missionaries. Hold up their hands in the work of the Lord. Encourage them in their tireless efforts. Speak words of sympathy and helpfulness and understanding. Refrain from being too judgmental.

There are those among us living today, for I have spoken to a few, who wish they could have a few moments with David Bobo so they could apologize for the wrong they did to the man. But he is where the accusers, and the accuser, can harm him no longer.

When I close my eyes and rememember real hard, I can almost hear him speaking now. "Won't you come to Jesus, as together we stand and sing?"

Good-bye, Jean

She was the mother of two bright and precious boys. Her husband was a wonderful deacon in a church where I once ministered. If ever I were to select a typical family that would represent all that is good and noble regarding Christian principles and commitment, it would have been this one. Jean was a wonderful example of Christian womanhood. Her devotion to her boys was legend. If I could level one charge against her, it was that her house was so neatly kept that it made anyone who visited think they had better tidy up a bit when they got back home. Her vice, if it can be called that, was that she was a neat freak. I'm sure her house could have withstood the white glove test at any given hour of the day or night. Some psychologist might come up with a sinister and deep obsessive compulsive diagnosis, but I think Jean just cared for her family and took her domestic responsibilities seriously.

Jean was also heavily involved in the ministries of the church. She was one of our best and most devoted Bible class teachers. Her classes were among the most popular with the children. She also taught foreign students, by way of correspondence courses, and was always involved in the benevolent outreach of the church. This Christian woman seemed joyful and fulfilled. Yet, one Wednesday evening, just after reading a story to her boys and sending them off to mid-week Bible class (she normally went with them), she wrote a short note to her husband who was working the night shift that evening, then she got into her car that was parked in the garage and started the engine. She had left the garage door and car windows down. Her husband found her lifeless form when he arrived home from work a short time later.

The shock to the church was overwhelming. Those who loved her were horrified that such a thing could happen right under their noses without a hint that something was wrong. The ones closest to her seemed to switch into some sort of slow motion, novocaine-like, stupor that helped them cope with their loss. The days that followed were among the most difficult in my minstry.

Life, even for the most optimistic Christian, living with the joyful certainty of eternity with God, is sometimes just bearable at best. Some of the fears and anxieties that haunt each of us are often only known by ourselves alone. We keep so much of our emotional stress hidden deep within. Of all the people on the planet whom I might have guessed to be suicidal, Jean would have been at the bottom of the list. And yet, here she was, dead at her own hands, leaving two young sons and a grieving husband to try to sort through what might have pushed her over the edge. And, of course, there was the immediate feeling of guilt by her mate. The question, "What did I do wrong?" or "How did I fail my wife?" must have leapt to the forefront of his mind. I surely had no glib answers. About all I could do for Ernie was to embrace him and weep with him.

Suicide is often a silent killer. It doesn't always announce itself with a calling card or letter of intent. For those who die in Christ, it was always a sort of celebration. I considered it a graduation to glory, if you please. Therefore I didn't dread participating in the funerals of Christians. But a funeral for someone who took her own life was quite a challenge for this young preacher. I had conducted a funeral, a year or two before this, of a young man who had been suffering from mental illness for years. He went home from work one evening, laid out his best clothes, took a shower, combed his hair, put on cologne, then picked up a shotgun and blew his brains out. It was a lot more understandable for the family because of the mental illness factor. It comforted them when I suggested that those who are not competent would be judged less severely for their behavior. But what does one say at the funeral of someone who was bright and seemingly happy with life but who, with much forethought and planning, designed her suicide down to the last detail?

I can't speak for other preachers, nor can I speak for other Christians, but I hold the conviction that when one commits suicide, she is not accountable for her actions. One of our strongest instincts is the will to survive; we struggle to live. On the very worst days of our lives, most of us will choose life over death. It seems to me that one must be temporarily out of his mind to commit that final violent act.

Satan is a death devil. He wishes to snuff out our influence for good and our witness for Christ. He thought that when Jesus was crucified it was his greatest victory. He must not have realized it was to be his greatest defeat. We die sometimes because the father of lies provokes some of us into thinking death is an adventure. Many of us die because we have failed to successfully resist the temptations to disobey our God. At a weak moment in her life, Satan sifted poor Jean as wheat and, she became a victim.

At the funeral, one sad soul uttered the most distasteful comment I have ever heard at such an occasion. He said to the grief stricken husband, "Ernie, you know you'll never see Jean again because she committed murder. And if you murder yourself, you can never be forgiven." Now, I can't be sure of what others might think of such consoling, but I think it's from Satan himself. It isn't even Biblical. If suicide is murder, even murderers can be forgiven. If not, Paul is in for a big surprise. Those who killed Jesus and then obeyed the gospel in penitence could not be forgiven if such were not so. And it seems to me to be mighty presumptuous to say that an otherwise normal, healthy and stable Christian woman who suddenly takes her life while in mental distress is comparable to her committing a murder.

The consolation I offered at the funeral was that Jean had been temporarily out of her mind and was, therefore, not accountable for her actions. I know a case for the other side could be argued. She planned it. She even wrote a good-bye note. But who can prove that premeditation always indicates one is in his right mind? So I don't worry about Jean much anymore. I believe the God of all the earth will do right by her. I am not endorsing nor condoning suicide as a viable option for Christians. But I am saying that even at our worst, God is always at His best.

My sister in Christ left us saddened and lonely for awhile. Yet, I hope with great expectation for her salvation and look to the day when she and all God's children will be united in that great eternal family. His mercy is great.

The Board of Education

His name was Kasimir A. Wykowsky. He was the principal of Margaret McFarland school #4 in Marion County, Indiana. For some reason he seemed to take a special liking to my sister and me. He gave me individual attention when I was struggling with my math. And, I remember, he wrote in cursive like some master of calligraphy. I was impressed. I tried to write just as neatly as he. And I almost had it mastered for a few years. But things change.

Mr. Wykowsky was also the enforcer at our school. If you misbehaved, the worst possible consequence was to be sent to his office. Right next to his desk he kept a long paddle made of oak. It was about a half inch thick with a cut out at the end to fit his hand. This, of course, was in the days of dinosaurs when teachers and administrators in schools could actually discipline their charges. Today, rather than the teachers threatening the children, the children threaten the teachers. This, of course, has kept the teachers "in line," allowing the children to pretty much run things as they wish. Unable to read and write, they sure can play some mean video games on the computers purchased by schools systems in order to be on the cutting edge of education. But, then again, that is a political issue and should not be in such a story as this.

Anyway, that paddle Mr. Wykowsky had hanging by his desk had beautifully hand-painted words on it. They looked so nice that I am sure Mr. Wykowsky had done the art work himself. The words were: "The Board of Education." All the kids knew what "The Board of Education" was for. It was like our politicians who wanted to keep us stockpiled in nuclear armaments. They called it a deterrent. And I suppose all those warheads were deterrents of a sort, for who in their right mind would want to unleash that kind of havoc on the world?

Most of the boys in my class had had some rather up close and personal acquaintance with "The Board of Education." It was meant to be a deterrent, but it didn't seem to work for everyone, until after their first experience with it. It worked for me from the start. That paddle had some sort of intimidating influence on my behavior as a student in the classroom. But, more importantly than that piece of oak wood, Mr. Wykowsky was a formidable deterrent. He held both teacher and student to a high standard of excellence. It showed in the way he dressed and in his meticulous penmanship. And I wanted to be like him.

Mr. Wykowsky was a mentor of mine, although I didn't understand that truth fully at the time. As years passed by I would occasionally see him. In the mall. At a grocery store or barber shop. He always remembered my name. I was flabbergasted at that. How could a principal with thousands of students in his career remember one lone kid's name? He would ask how my sister was, mentioning her by name, and also ask about my parents by name. He must have had a photographic mind or something. For some mysterious reason, and it is hard to fathom since I was quite a talker and cutup in the classroom, I escaped the sting of the "board." But I didn't escape the example of Mr. Wykowski. His standard of excellence impressed my boyish mind. His life was one of order and direction. He set a tone for the other teachers to emulate. And it spilled over into the studentry.

One other thing I appreciate about Mr. Wykowski is that he ran a school where kids learned to read and write and do their math. He hadn't yet learned all the new and innovative learning theories of the great educators of our day. He was a nuts and bolts administrator who was allowed the threat of corporal punishment to hang on his office wall. And with that power he helped mold and shape young lives for future excellence and success. He's gone on to his reward by now, but his memory lives on in the mind of at least this student. And as long as that memory lives, he will live. What a wonderful man. What a magnificent educator!

Doctor West

He was Jewish. I inherited him along with the family political party. He was a part of the Goad's inner circle, even before I made my first appearance on the scene of life. My life became intertwined with his before I was even born, and if my mother had taken his advice as seriously as she normally did, I might not have been able to tell you about this man. You see, Harold J. West was the family doctor.

I'm thankful I was born when I was. I could have been born before penicillin and might not have made it to my 25th birthday. I could have been born during the black plague and never got off the breast. Perhaps I could have been born in the '80s or '90s with the challenge of growing older in a society where the media delivers body counts of dead teens caused from drive-by shootings. Having been born in the decade of the '40s allowed me to experience the blessing of doctor's house calls. Harold still made house calls, especially if the Goad children were ill.

Dr. West saved my mother's life after he delivered my older sister. It was a difficult labor and life sapping birth. Mom lost so much blood that those in attendance thought they had lost her during the course of the delivery. But, alas, she lived long enough to ignore Dr. West's admonition that she dare not have any more children. Normally she would have followed his advice to the letter. She had complete trust in this man, with the lives of her children, and her own life as well.

I hated to go to the doctor's office. Ear problems found me often in his examining room. I didn't like to be examined. I didn't like to be probed and poked. I hated having that black rubber ball with a tube poking out of it being put in my ears and then squeezed like a bellows. It hurt. Why would a grown man want to hurt a little kid in the first place? He would squeeze air into my ears and ask me to say "raisins." I hated raisins. To this very moment raisins remind me of Dr. West. Raisins are nothing more than shriveled up grapes. Dr. West was like that. At 5 feet 1 inch, he looked like a shriveled up man. So we called him "Raisin man."

It was cruel, but it wasn't done in hate. We loved our family doctor and treated him as if he actually were one of the family.

I have forgotten the number of times my sister and I were either in his office or he was at our house because of fevers and chicken pox and mumps and measles and such. I still vividly recall the fevers associated with our vaccinations. Of course, I associated Dr. West with being sick, so I frankly didn't like him coming around the house. Not that I was inhospitable. On the contrary, I was about as hospitable as a kid my age could get. I mean, I was always inviting the neighborhood kids over for lunch and stuff. One day, Dr. West just happened to be in the neighborhood, and dropped by the house. The first thing I asked Mom was, "Who's sick?"

Dr. West prided himself as a healer. With his tongue depressors and bottles of liquids and pills, he was able to get all of us through the various diseases and conditions that prey on families such as ours. I didn't know much about Judaism at the time I was growing up. I remember mother sharing the gospel of Christ one day with Dr. West. She had tears in her eyes as I recall. He had handily rejected mother's attempt at converting him. Dad had little respect for the Jewish faith and let us know it from time to time. But one day, as I was attempting to get over the jitters of being stuck one more time with one of his needles, I started singing, "Jesus loves me this I know. For the Bible tells me so."

Dr. West started singing along with me. He knew every word of the song. I didn't realize I was singing a Jewish song. And I wondered if the good doctor knew that Jesus was a Jew. Surely he did. How could he have known that song?

No wonder our Savior tells us older ones to become like little children. Kids aren't prejudiced like adults. Oh, they might say what is on their mind. Kids say politically incorrect things at times. Things like "Why is that woman fat?" or "That man smells funny." or "Why is the preacher so boring?" or "Dr. West, Dad says you charged too much for that last house call." I may have been guilty of that last family secret being aired at the wrong time. As a minister, while visiting one home, a three-year-old climbed up on my lap and said out loud for all to hear, "Preacher, Daddy had to sleep on the couch last night!" Anyway, in my innocence I thought all adults loved Jesus. Whether one was a Jewish physician or a Buddhist dog catcher, I just assumed that everyone had been told about Christ and they all were smart enough to love Him as much as I did.

Mom took it especially hard when she got the news. Dr. West had shot himself in the head and was gone. It was like losing a family member. She wept at the news, for she was sure that he was slowly accepting the good news of a Savior. She had hopes that he would have accepted Christ and obeyed the gospel. He had always told her that he never wanted to lose his independence and become feeble. Before taking his own life, he had suffered a stroke that left him partially paralyzed. He felt himself a burden on his wife and family. I wish he had listened more closely to mother. Had he done so, he could have known that he was just as important to us and just as loved by us as he had been before the stroke. And I know one other thing for sure; Jesus, Harold's older Jewish brother, loved him, too.

Eugenia

Her name was Georgia Eugenia Coop-Goad. Coop was her maiden name. She grew up in the Cumberland Gap area of southern Kentucky. Dale Hollow Lake now occupies the land on which her father had his farm. The dam that some bureaucrats built close by created a marvelous fishing lake, but destroyed her growing up neighborhood. As Thomas Wolfe would say, "Eugenia, you can't go home again."

Why the name Georgia was avoided I do not know. Perhaps she preferred the name Eugenia. All of her friends called her Jean or Jeanie. My father never called her Georgia, so I didn't know my mother's name was Georgia or Eugenia until I got old enough to care about such details. The important thing was that I called her "Mom," and a finer mother a boy could never find. God's providence plopped me right smack dab in the middle of the life of Jeanie Goad, and I have never stopped thanking Him for the privilege of being her son.

She was a beautiful woman, physically and spiritually. She was, as so many boys discover about their moms, my first love. I was proud when people complimented her on her beauty. Harry Davis, who is now 94 and still recalls mother's charm, told me that she could cut a hole in a sheet, put her head through it, tie a rope around her waist and still look better than all the other women in the world. Harry isn't a man to exaggerate.

What a marvelously positive impact she made on the lives of my sister and me. She was a country girl who learned to live in the big city and behave accordingly. Always eager to share her faith in God at work or play, it was she who taught me my first memory passages from Scripture. It was she who taught me how to pray before going to bed at night. It was she who developed in me my gentler graces that surface from time to time.

Occasionally kids at school would have forgotten something and their mothers would bring whatever it was to class. Some of those mothers looked like they had been sitting inside a dryer before showing up at the classroom. One day I forgot my lunch.

Most kids were embarrassed when their parents showed up at school, whatever the reason. Not me. My mom marched into the classroom (I was in 5th grade) and asked Mrs. Henzie if she could give me my sack lunch. It usually held a sandwich, a banana, if I were lucky a Twinkie or Snowball, and a homemade cookie or two. The other kids couldn't take their eyes off mother. When she left, one of the boys said, "Wow! Who was that?" I gladly announced that she was my mother. "She's the prettiest girl I've ever seen." The buttons almost popped off my shirt.

Something happened when I was sixteen that I have had a lover's quarrel with God about ever since. Mom died. Her crossing over wasn't sudden, but came only after a lingering and humiliating illness that robbed her not only of her beauty, but sapped her energy as well. The last thing the cancer took from her was her will to live. The doctor said that if it hadn't been for her strong heart and will, she would have died much earlier. She was my guiding star and I didn't discover the fullness of that truth until she was taken from us. I thought I was a tough guy back then. Now I realize that I was just a kid who needed his mother desperately.

Dad was magnificent at keeping some semblance of order to our lives during her extended illness. I was incapable of understanding it at the time, but there were tremendous pressures on my father. Not only was he suffering the emotional trauma of seeing his beloved mate wasting away day by day, but the financial pressures were there as well. The doctor bills must have been horrendous. But that was never discussed in my hearing, and for that sense of stability, I thank my father.

One evening in particular stands out in my mind as I recall mother. It was a few days before she left us. It was one of the few occasions during the final days of her illness where she was lucid and able to communicate. The pain killers had left her, I am sure, addicted. We all gathered around her bed. She wept as she said, "I just wanted you all to know how much I love my family." She repeated this several times as I recall. I thought it must have been the drugs. But, on reflection, I am convinced she was deliberate in repeating herself. She was making sure we understood. It was a final gathering of the clan and a last farewell. We wept, too. Unabashedly. Unashamedly. Copiously. My sister, Jackie, and I knew we were losing something more precious than gold. Dad was literally losing a part of himself. It was the saddest occasion in all of my life. God released dear mother from her prison of pain a few days afterwards.

That night, by Mom's bed, she asked the three of us to always remain faithful to the Lord. We all promised. Many times, in weakness and in stark rebellion, I broke that promise. I'm trying desperately now to keep it. Her memory lends support to the effort. The best things parents can give impressionable youngsters is to allow Christ to be seen in them. Mom surely did that for me. The best that children can give back to their parents is to honor and obey them in the Lord. May I always repay her in kind.

It was a Wednesday evening when mother crossed over into paradise. I was at Bible class, where she would have wanted me to be, when I got the call. I had gone to my place of employment to get my paycheck that afternoon. I was running behind schedule so rushed home and threw on my church clothes. For some reason I didn't go, as I usually did, into her room and kiss her forehead and tell her I loved her. Oh, the crystal clear vision of hindsight! I've berated myself for it ever since.

There was a knock on the door of the classroom. We were about halfway through the lesson. A dear elder stood at the door and asked to see me. He looked extremely sad. He had a hard time telling me the news. "Stevie," he began. Then a tear came to his eye and his chin began to tremble. He didn't have to say it. I knew what he was going to tell me. My heart sank. "Stevie," he started again, "Your father wants you to come home now. Your mother has passed away."

What a simple sentence. "Your mother has passed away." Those were the most difficult five words I have ever heard. I wanted to hit something or someone. I was mad. I didn't even cry at first. I started to run down the hallway and the elder grabbed me and asked, "Are you going to be okay?" I don't remember if I answered him or not. I just bounded for the door and got into my car and made the longest journey of my life. It was only a few miles home, but they were the dreariest and loneliest miles I had ever traveled.

I talked to God as I was driving. It was more like talking "at" God. I knew she was dying, but I had also known I was praying for her to get well. So much of my monologue (I wasn't about to let Him get a word in edgewise) with God that trip was telling Him what I thought of Him not answering my prayer in a proper manner. I was mad. I was questioning my Maker, the one who had gifted me with such a perfect mother. I was crossing the White River bridge on Raymond Street when my anger turned into tears. I started crying so profusely that I couldn't see to drive.

I literally had to turn to the side of the road and stop the car. I have no idea how long I sat there and wept. But I needed the tears. They cleansed my eyes of anger and cleansed my heart of malice toward my Heavenly Father. Jesus wept. Steven wept. I cried even more at the funeral later, but those tears, by myself, in my car, were the bitterest and most cathartic tears of my life.

If anyone else had been around, I might have been embarrassed. I was sobbing like a little kid. Deep, convulsive sobs. And I couldn't seem to stop the waterworks. Then, from a Source I had forgotten for awhile, God gave me strength. I did what I had always done while sitting next to mother in church. I sang. I started haltingly, "O, Lord my God. . . . ."

It wasn't just a song, it was an apology to God for chewing Him out for what He had done to my family. "When I in awesome wonder, consider all the worlds Thy hands have made." I had been singing at the top of my lungs. When I had finished the last chorus, my eyes were dry and I had regained my composure. I wanted to be strong for Dad when I got home. If I felt such great loss, imagine what my father must have felt.

Singing is good for the soul. It isn't a mistake that God asks us to sing. I recommend it. It has gotten me through many a difficult evening. When memories flood of heartache and disappointment, singing reaffirms His love for me. When I am glad, singing helps me remember how blessed I have been. I've already lived on the planet ten years longer than mother had. She was so young.

And it isn't fair. Life isn't fair. God never said it would be. But eternity will be fair. God, in His beneficent superintending of the universe, allows it to rain on the just and the unjust. And so shall it ever be until that great day of accounting.

The greatest gift to children is righteous parents. If you are reading this and your parents are still alive, go to them and embrace them and tell them you love them. Call them on the phone. Don't wait until it's too late. Do it now. And if you are a parent, be to your children what God created you to be. Nurture them. Guide them. Set an example of righteous excellence that they can emulate. Do for them what Georgia Eugenia did for me.

Chapter Seven

Sentimental Journeys

Under New Management

It was one of the best places in town to eat. The menu was simple and not written in some foreign language. The lighting was bright enough so you could read the prices. And the food was excellent. The owners had spent several years building up the reputation of their business. They gave hearty portions and kept close watch over the quality of each food item. Word of mouth got most of their business for them. They rarely had to advertise.

Sadly, family troubles and health problems forced them to sell. Within weeks the restaurant was in trouble. The portions were smaller. The quality of the food slipped. Instead of a parking lot full of cars, it often stood empty. I quit eating there. Old customers were disappointed as they, one by one, took their business elsewhere. The proprietors soon filed for bankruptcy and, again, the business changed hands. The new owners, apparently in an attempt to attract some former customers, put up a sign: "Under New Management." Being the optimist that I am, I gave it another try. I was delighted with the food and the service. My faith was renewed.

A few years ago I attended my 25th high school class reunion. It was amazing how old some of my former friends looked. One of the guys, who had been most obnoxious back in school, was in attendance. But there was something glaringly different about him. It wasn't just his hairline. His personality seemed different. It was as though I was talking with an entirely different person. One thing I immediately noticed was that his foul mouth had disappeared. His gruff and insulting manner had been replaced by a charismatic gentlemanliness. How could this be? Sensing something I might be delighted to learn, I got up the courage to ask him what had happened in his life. He answered with a smile. "Steve, I'm under new management." He went on to explain how Christ had become the moving force in his life.

Know what? When we discover that our lives are full of sin, and realize our separation from God, and then find out we can change all of that for the good by giving our lives to Christ, we can act upon that knowledge and we really do put ourselves under new management. We no longer attempt to manage our own affairs by trial and error. We now have perfect help. The word of God becomes a guiding influence in our everyday routines. The mundane becomes the sublime.

New management makes a difference in the world of business and the world of sinners. The good news of Jesus is that we can have a fresh start. When the Spirit of Christ comes in to dwell, we can be assured that the new has arrived and the old way of doing things is history.

Jesus can change a drunk into a loving father and husband. He can create a loving mother out of a crack addict. The Lord can turn a tyrannical boss into a considerate mentor, an arrogant know-it-all into a humble servant, a marriage on the rocks into a lifetime commitment, a dysfunctional family with kids ruling the roost into a model of how God's powerful love can change hearts.

Have you considered such a change in management? Do it! It will give you a whole new lease on life. Better still, it will give you an insight, and an entrée, into eternity.

The Preciousness of Life

Life is so fragile. Occasionally we are awestruck at how much abuse the human body can experience and still survive; yet in another sense, it doesn't take much to traumatize our physical existence and snap us into eternity. And when our loved ones are taken from us, we don't take it lightly. We mourn, and all but deny their departure.

One day in particular I was struck with the uncertainty of life, with how easily it can be taken from us. It was a typically hot and humid day in Mobile, Alabama. My eldest son was walking home from school. He was in the first grade and only had to walk a block from the school yard to his front yard.

Our street wasn't particularly heavily traveled. We had our share of cars, and since it was a residential area, most drivers were cautious and rarely sped. But on this day events were set in motion that almost culminated in tragedy.

Why we fear the death of our children more than any other death is a mystery. It ought to give us hope when little ones are taken from us. And, in one sense, we are hopeful when little ones die because we know of their innocence. But there is a special kind of hurt attached to losing our young children. We can more easily let go of grandma or grandpa. They have enjoyed full lives. But for a six-year-old child to be prematurely snatched from our arms is more difficult than just about any grief we encounter.

Matthew was quite a runner. He loved to run. He was faster than most of the kids his age. We had warned him as best we could about not crossing streets without looking both ways. But on this particular day he was excited about a project he had done at school. He was anxious to show it to us. He was hurrying as fast as his little feet could carry him to his house on McRae Avenue.

I was in the front yard as he was excitedly approaching our house. I cannot recall a day in my life when I was more frightened and more thankful, all at the same moment. It was truly a case of mixed emotions. It surpassed the day I almost drowned while still a boy, not much older than Matthew was at the time of this incident. Matthew caught my eye as he ran down the sidewalk toward our home. He was on the opposite side of the street and had to stop and look both ways and then dash across to our house. He forgot to look. All he could think about was getting a hug from me and showing me his art work. What a fine little artist he was, too.

I could see it coming. It was almost like watching something in slow motion. He made his turn and ran toward the street just as a car came racing past at high speed. He was unaware of the car. I screamed at the top of my lungs, "Matthew, stop!!" He was an obedient son, and I thank God to this day for it. He stopped immediately as the car caught his art work and tore his shirt. He was that close to being catapulted into eternity.

After the car was gone Matthew could only stand in place, motionless, rigid, trembling at the thought of having come that close to dying. Even his youthful age allowed him to catch the horror of it. I raced to him with mixed emotions. I was angry that he had almost sacrificed himself to stupidity, but elated that God's providence had spared his life. I ran to him and scooped him up in my arms. I shouted a few admonitions in my sternest voice about remembering to look before crossing any street, then I broke down in tears. We both cried. I was never more thankful for my children than at that moment.

All parents can probably tell stories of close calls. I have many friends who have lost their children to various accidents and diseases. And somehow, with God's mercy, I could have survived the mourning of a lost son if that had been the result of this encounter with an automobile. But God spared Matthew for something. He is a commercial artist today. I love to see his handiwork still. I've saved the ripped art work that was torn from his hand that day to remind me of how precious life really is. And I get mad when I hear of parents abusing their little ones and taking them for granted.

Don't wait for some tragedy, or near tragedy, to occur. Go to your children; go to your mates; go to your parents;

embrace them and tell them how much they mean to you. Do it soon, because we never know when we will see each other for the last time in this life. But, thanks to Jesus, Christians will never see each other for the *last* time.

Friendship

It is axiomatic that to have a friend one must be a friend. And I'm convinced at this point in my life that friendship is among life's most treasured blessings. Everybody needs at least one friend. It can be your mate or a neighbor or an old school chum. Most of us need lots of friends to make life most enjoyable. So I've chosen to have several "best" friends over the years.

Each friendship is a story in itself. I could write an entire book on the life and times of Stevie Goad and Ronnie Kelp. We both had funny last names. We were inseparable in our grammar school days. One day we'd be mad at each other and the next we'd be best buddies again. We took an Indian blood brother vow to be bachelors all our lives and thus eliminate any close proximity to those silly females who were afraid of frogs and mice. He lasted to the end of his nineteenth year before marrying my favorite grade school sweetheart, Barbara. I still look Ronnie up on occasion when I visit my old home town.

Then there was that unique servant of God during my ministry in southern Indiana. He was a deacon while I was serving there. He grew into one of God's fine elders. He was my tennis partner and my sounding board. Hayward Blanton became the brother I never had. He could do no wrong in my eyes. Nor could I in his. We worked side by side as co-laborers in the body of Christ. We fed on each other's encouragement. Ah, Christian friends are especially memorable.

Jere Allan is my present "best" friend. He is like an older brother to me. Also an elder in the church, Jere has come to my aid so many times I have lost count. He has defended me at times when I was wrongfully accused. He has encouraged me when I was down and depressed. Never have I known a man more respected in his community and about whom no unkind word is ever spoken, nor ever is heard even a hint of impropriety. If the church had more men the likes of Jere Brett Allan, there would surely be fewer preacher moves each summer.

What would we do without friends? I know what some people do. They "look for love in all the wrong places." They become addicted to drugs of choice that numb their loneliness and mask their desperation. They commit suicide. In God's divine providence, no one need be friendless. Abraham was called the friend of God. All of us can be God's friends. Jesus is a friend who can be relied upon and who will not disappoint. And He provides a family of friends in His church.

The way to achieve friendship with God is to refuse to be a "friend to the world." The lust of the flesh, the lust of the eye and the pride of life goad us into friendship with the world. But it isn't worth the effort.

The song "What A Friend We Have In Jesus" testifies to the availability of Christ. In the making of friends, even "best" friends, don't forget to be a friend to God. Obey Him. Seek His advice. Thank Him for the other close relationships you enjoy with fellow believers. And remind yourself occasionally that the closest friend of all, the most loyal friend of all, is only a prayer away.

Buckwheat

My youngest son, Marc, was still living at home. I had been away visiting my sick father back in Indiana. So it was Marc's decision, not mine. He should have known better. I had told him repeatedly that he would have to be more responsible when making decisions that involved the outlay of money or that would entail the continual need of our time and attention. And this was surely one of the those decisions.

When I arrived home, I was confronted with one of Marc's choices that I somehow knew would be funded from my account. She had already been given a name: Buckwheat.

Dogs have a way of tugging at my heartstrings. For years I had been hard-nosed about getting another dog. It wasn't that I disliked them. It was the other way around. I found that I became so attached to them that they began ruling my life. Vacations were planned around family dogs. Budgets were planned around unexpected veterinary bills. Affections had to be doled out to family members, if any were left after giving most away to the mutts that had become family members, too.

Dogs were a part of my growing up. Sadly, I didn't seem to be able to keep a dog for over a year or two. Some I only had for a few months. They were victims of hit-and-run drivers, poison, distemper, and other canine enemies.

My first dog was named Sparky. He was sent prematurely to doggy heaven for killing our laying hens. I was mad at Dad for weeks over that. Then there were Specs (he had rings around his eyes that looked just like glasses), Rusty, Bootsie, Candy, Topsy, Captain Blondie and maybe some others along the way of my boyhood years. When they were taken from me, it was the hardest thing I could do to get over them. I loved them more than I did people. They didn't hurt me and hold grudges and do bad things like people sometimes did.

In my marriage years there were Lucky, Lady, Schotzie, Misty and another Lady (a black cocker that we actually had for years and years). Lady had been abandoned in the middle of a hard winter with her little puppies. She was hard to rescue because of her tenacity at protecting her litter. When she finally had to be put to sleep, blind, deaf and riddled with tumors, we might as well have lost one of the family. For she had literally become one of us. I was determined that that kind of hurt was never going to be allowed in my life again, not if I could help it. As much as I adored puppies, their sad eyes weren't going to capture my devotion. And I succeeded in this stubbornness for several years. I shouldn't have left town, I suppose.

It was a friend who took advantage of Marcus while I was gone. She brought over the cutest little sandy colored cur you ever laid your eyes on. Had I been there, I would have said, "No! Absolutely not. No way, José! Nada. Nyet! The dog is outta here!!"

But Marc is a sucker for a pretty face. This little puppy had the saddest eyes. Above her eyes were literal, human-like, dark eyebrows, slightly slanted, kinda like John Wayne's, that made you feel sorry for her. Add to that the fact that she had been abandoned and needed a home; Marc couldn't help himself. "Sure, we'll be glad to take her. I know Dad will love her as much as I will."

When I arrived home from my trip, I was livid that a dog was taking up residence in my house, without my permission. I tried as I may to get up the gumption to have Marc take the puppy back to the one who brought it to us, but the more I held her and the more I smelled that sweet puppy's breath and the longer I gazed into those eyes, the more certain it became that I was hooked.

Buckwheat now, more or less, runs the household. She is as big as a horse (why didn't someone tell me she was a German Shepherd and Chow mix?). She eats three large cans of expensive wet dog food a day (my Scotch genes resist this outlay of cash with much trepidation and guilt). She is a tick magnet and has cost me an arm and a toe at the vets. But, my goodness, what a fine looking dog she turned out to be. Everyone admires her confirmation and her gentle ways. And I am sure she is a far better alarm system than I could have installed electronically. So, here she is, one of the Goads. She's already been written into the will.

One day, while the family was away, Buckwheat got out of the yard. At least we thought she got out. We know not how. The gate had been latched and her yard was bordered by a six foot high wooden fence. We were frantic. We scoured the neighborhood for hours. We combed the entire town. We couldn't find her. We made Lost Dog signs and posted them all over town, at ATM machines, at the post office, at the laundry and dry cleaners, at businesses and on telephone poles. We were one sad family.

On Sunday morning, just as I was dressed and had 20 minutes to spare to get to my morning Bible class, we got the call. This will sound heretical to die-hard churchgoers, but I asked one of my elders to take my place teaching adult Bible class. "Are you sick, Steve?" "No, brother Jere. Someone called and told me they think they saw our dog." Only one of God's special elders would have understood such a request. Someone had seen one of our signs at an ATM. "I think I saw the dog you are hunting for," she told my wife. "It had a blue collar like was in the description. But she's across the river in Glenberg."

We live in a small desert town just west of the Blackfoot River. Glenberg is across the river. How Buckwheat could have gotten all the way across the river to Glenberg has been a mystery. We think someone stole her. If you could see her you would understand why. So here we were, my wife Laura and I, driving into some lagoon area of the river fully dressed for church. It was hot, maybe 110 degrees or so. We had been looking for so long for our beloved pet that we didn't really think this trip would be fruitful, especially miles away from home and across a river. We drove slowly all around the spot where the caller had said she had last seen her. We repeatedly called out her name. We had used up most of our Bible class time in the search and were just about ready to give up the effort when I made one last appeal. "Buckwheat! Here, girl! Here, Buckwheat!!"

Out from the waters of the lagoon shot a large sandy head. Her ears were normally asymmetrical. But at this moment in time, she had both ears, even the floppy one, standing at full attention. I almost didn't recognize her. Normally, with the floppy ear configuration, she looks a bit like Marmaduke. But that day she looked like a trained police dog. I called her name once again and you should have seen the speed with which she emerged from the water. And then she galloped, and I use the word advisedly because of her size, as fast as her hoofs, I mean pasterns, could carry her. She had been swimming in the slimy lagoon water and now her wet fur was picking up gobs of sand and dirt and filth as she bolted toward us. She had a long way to run. And the closer she got, the more concerned we became. We hadn't planned on anything quite like this. I had on a brand new Bill Blass suit. Laura was in one of her pretty white dresses. Can you picture what happened next? That's right. I did what any red-blooded American male chauvinist would do, I jumped into the car and rolled up the windows as fast as I could. And it wasn't a moment too soon. Seconds later Buckwheat bounded happily, all 90 pounds of her, into Laura's waiting arms. It was quite a reunion indeed.

For a fastidious parson, the mud didn't seem to make me as upset as I would normally get. There was mud everywhere. All over Buckwheat. All over Laura's pretty dress. In the car. But not on my new suit. Nosiree! It was a messy occasion, but a happy one.

There is no real end to a story like this, because it's not really a story. It's more like a confession. It's an admission of how much God's animals mean to those of us who have learned to love them as though they were also created in His image. I hope you have enjoyed this tale of one dog that is enjoying the love and affection that I also shared with all those marvelous mutts who came before her.

It was a little embarrassing shuffling into the church house for worship. We got a lot of teasing about being out dog hunting instead of being in Bible class. But later it dawned on me that Jesus left the ninety and nine that safely lay in the shelter of the fold, and went to look for the one that was lost. Yes, I know the sheep represented a human soul, but Buckwheat represented love and protection and forgiveness.

Whether we have time for her or not, she always has plenty of time for us. When we treat her badly, which isn't often, she has never held a grudge. So, was I really violating the spirit of the passage in Luke 15? I think not. And may God continue to bless this amazing living creature by the name of Buckwheat, a sweet friend on loan from God who has learned to love the Goad family, warts and all.

"Here, Buckwheat! Good girl."

The Laying On of Hands

It was sweltering that summer, just south of Burksville, Kentucky as we were vacationing at Dale Hollow Lake. Dad was helping Grandpa Coop get his fishing cabins in order for the next wave of fishermen. Dad and I were sort of helping Grandpa with his business and enjoying the lake at the same time. It was a working vacation.

Have you ever seen something that was so hilarious that you could hardly contain your laughter, but had to hold it back because it would offend others? Or maybe the one that was causing the humor took himself too seriously and would have had his feelings hurt? This was the case that day when my beloved sire had to practice the sudden laying on of hands.

We were working on a barbecue that Dad was making out of bricks. They were old used bricks that had been laying in a pile for years awaiting Grandpa's urge to work. He had always talked of making a place for the fishermen to cook out at night. So Dad was doing his best, with questionable masonry skills at hand, to help Pa Coop realize his barbecue.

Just about every other brick had a scorpion hiding under it. We were being very cautious while picking up each brick, making sure that we kicked it first and then carefully lifted it with gloved hands. Aunt Adgie had even found a scorpion in one of the fishing cabins, right in the middle of a bed, between the sheets. So, we were all a little on edge regarding creepy-crawly things.

A lot of people were coming and going. Fishermen were docking their boats. We were close to a floating general store that Bee Wyatt, a fixture in those parts, operated. So, at any given moment there were several people at hand. Just as Dad was about to pick up another brick to put in place, he shouted out an ear-splitting, blood-curdling scream the likes of which I had not heard before, or since. This was the moment in time when Dad began to practice the laying on of hands.

It is amazing what we can do when we are scared. We lose all the social graces. We think of nothing and no one except survival. Now, the Goad family was a modest family. We just didn't go out in public unless we were properly attired. Why, even in our own congregation we had been lectured from the pulpit that it was a sin to go mixed bathing at public pools. I guessed they called it "bathing" to make it sound so much more sinful. Because, frankly, I never did take a bar of soap with me when I sneaked to the swimming pool with Ronnie Kelp.

Anyway, Dad grabbed hold of his pants legs and started hopping around on one foot like a one-legged man on a pogo stick.

We had been preached to that it was a sin to dance. I mean, it was wrong to dance, period. Dancing was forbidden in our fellowship. But I had to admit that I hadn't seen any dance in all my life quite like the one my father was doing at that moment.

Dad had taken hold of his pants leg with both hands and seemed to be in a bit of trouble. Everyone seemed aware of trouble, but nobody knew exactly what was wrong. Finally Dad quit jumping up and down and dancing a jig and rested on his one leg with the other extended forward. He very carefully let loose of the pant leg with one hand and unbuckled his belt. I said, "Dad, what are you doing?" He said nothing as he unzipped his trousers and let them drop down to where his other hand was holding onto the leg.

Slowly, methodically, he carefully opened his hand to reveal a poor little lizard that had sacrificed himself to Dad's terror of the scorpion. Dad had thought he was about to be stung by a scorpion and he didn't relish the thought of that stinging creature making any more headway up his leg than he already had. To Dad's relief, he flipped the lizard onto the ground and sat down on a tree stump to gain his composure. He didn't even take time to pull his pants back up.

Poor Pappy! He could have had a heart attack. He could have fallen down and hurt himself. Worse, he could have actually had a scorpion up his leg and got the sting of his life. And, as an obedient and faithful son, I sat down beside him and stifled a grin. Then I stifled a laugh. Have you ever tried to completely contain a 100 megaton laugh? I started to spit. Then I sputtered. Then it all came gushing out. I was afraid to laugh because I knew Dad would give me a good one for appearing to be so disrespectful and unconcerned. But I couldn't help myself. It was the funniest thing I had ever seen in my life. It was much better than a Jerry Lewis film.

Guess what? Instead of giving me a whack with his belt, I mean it was handy and all with his pants already undone, he started laughing, too. And we laughed until we cried. And we laughed until our sides hurt. And nobody can ever convince me that that wasn't the best vacation of my life. Laughter is good for the soul.

Learn to laugh at yourself. Learn to give up the somber, morose, life-is-full-of-heartache attitude and have a good belly laugh now and then. . . . .at yourself. I'll never forget the day my father laid hands suddenly on a poor gecko lizard, thus providing the scenario for the funniest moment of my life. It still hurts to think about it.

On Teasing

I grew up in a family of teasers. Teasing is ingrained in my personality. So, I joke a lot. It has gotten me into lots of trouble over the years. Sadly, people with chips on their shoulders don't like to be teased. On a bad hair day, I might not even like it. Thus, conflict ensues. The maddest I've seen anyone in my life was a fellow "Christian" I mistakenly teased. What anger and malice spewed forth from that poor soul.

On one particular summer day my little gang of playmates discovered the price of pulling the wrong kind of prank. We had a motley crew of neighborhood boys that were loosely thrown together simply because of geographical proximity. This pool of diverse genetic produce was an amalgamation of different temperaments and shapes and sizes and dispositions. Sort of like a mini-church. After all, church throws people together who, under other circumstances, might not have even spoken to one another. Yet, such people find themselves intimately entwined in the affairs of each other as they labor together for the cause of Christ. Strangers become family. Thus became our little club. And we had our own baptismal entrance into the fellowship. There were about twelve of us altogether for the duration of how long it would take to grow up in suburban Indianapolis. Now it seems we grew up too fast.

But that day we surely didn't behave as grownups. We were in an impish mood. We were in the mood to tease and wanted to pull a trick on one of the new kids on the block. We were known for teasing one another to the point of fights. Today we would pick on Billy, the boy who had just moved into the red brick house on the corner. One might call it his initiation into the fellowship. We wanted to test his mettle and see what he was made of. We didn't want to just allow any old new kid on the block into our brotherhood. So we set him up.

We had an old swimming hole that we often used for keeping cool when the humidity got above 150 percent. It was part of Bean Creek which ran through the heart of our turf. It was a perfectly secluded place, far from the madding crowd, a place for mischievous little boys to congregate, and a place to plan our future and discuss the past. Of all our meeting places, this was the best.

There were swinging vines hanging from tall trees surrounding the water hole. We would swing out as far as we could, yell Geronimo, and splash happily into the cool water. But that summer day it would become a place of horror and sadness for a bunch of kids who hadn't yet learned that life could be more serious than silly.

We took Billy to the secret spot. Just allowing him to be in our special place was an acknowledgment that we had accepted him into our little circle. But we wanted to be sure he had the kind of stuff, whatever this undefined and non-verbalized "stuff" really was, that could tolerate the myriad of warped personalities in our cadre of kids. We told him to swing out on one of the vines and let go. I mean, if a kid wasn't brave enough to do that, we didn't want him hanging around us. We didn't cotton to no sissies in our fellowship. Nosiree!

It's sad what we make each other do to be accepted. We bind heavy weights on others that they shouldn't have to bear. Like the Pharisees of Jesus' day, we load large burdens upon them and then will not so much as lend a finger to steady the load. We want women to be a certain size and shape. We want men to keep from crying. Stiff upper lip and all. We want people to dress the way we dress, smell the way we smell and not talk with an accent. We have great expectations of one another and then are quick to judge, quick to scorn, quick to reject those who don't meet our standard of behavior or appearance. And it's wrong. Painfully wrong.

Billy had such a bright smile on his face that day. He was elated that his first week in the neighborhood found him among so many new friends. What he didn't know is that he had been set up. We weren't really his friends that day. We were more his nemeses. What we hadn't told Billy was that the drought had caused the creek to run very dry, and when it did, that the swimming hole was dangerously shallow.

Nobody had ever gotten seriously hurt there, even when it was shallow, so it hadn't dawned on us that our unsuspecting victim could harm himself, other than maybe have his dignity tarnished a bit. But then he'd see that we were all laughing and would enjoy the joke as much as we. The worst that could happen would be that he might stub a toe on one of the many rocks that lined the base of our pool. Or, so we thought.

Billy was a daring lad. He had more guts than the rest of us combined. Each time one of us had been "initiated," we had cautiously and sheepishly swung out and sort of belly flopped into the water. But not Billy. He took a running leap and swung as far out as he could, he even went past the center of the pool and almost to the other side. On his return backward he let out a mighty yell that made us all proud. Then he let go of the vine and dove head first into the creek.

I don't know who was first in the water when we saw that he didn't immediately come to the surface with a smile on his face saying what we all had said before, "Wow, that's fun!" Billy had broken his neck. He was paralyzed from the neck down. The doctors told his parents he would be a quadriplegic the rest of his life. And nothing we could do would undo what a simple boyhood episode of teasing had done to our new friend. All of us have lived with the memory of that infamous summer day stamped indelibly on our minds. I don't know how the other fellows have dealt with it, but I still suffer from guilt for having been part of it.

A dear brother in Christ recently apologized to me for teasing me so much. He said, more or less, "Steve, I don't mean anything by it." I responded, "I take from it that it means you love me." For, you see, we really only tease those we love. We don't poke fun at strangers, at least not to their faces. We don't tease our enemies. Not us Christians. We have learned better. We tease and have fun with and bedevil each other. Why? Because we love each other, that's why.

To this very day I'm suspicious of those who never tease me. Makes me wonder if they really care. Makes me think they might be my enemies. One of my worst enemies never said an unkind word to me, nor ever did me dirty to my face.

But I found out later that he despised me and did whatever underhanded thing he could to discredit me, behind my back, of course.

By teasing, we are not suggesting a continual onslaught of rude joking or dangerous set-ups at another's expense. We surely are not writing of parental behavior that provokes children to anger. When we irritate and torment others, the fun and lightheartedness vanishes. The mean-spiritedness becomes obvious. Being teased, at least to me, is sort-o-like a mini roast. We don't roast people we don't like.

One point I wish to make is for children of God to lighten up a bit. Don't take yourself so seriously that you can't laugh at yourself. Quit wearing your feelings on your sleeve. Paradoxically, often those who tease the most accept it the least. Why that is, I don't fully understand. Perhaps it's because their so-called teasing isn't teasing at all, but true feelings couched in barbs.

Friends! Oh, to be blessed with so many in Jesus. Teasing, accepting, loving, silly, serious friends. Billy was my friend. He still is. I surely didn't want our friendship to cost as much as it did. And I'm sorry. Billy, I'm sorry that my way of showing my acceptance cost you so dearly. Forgive me.

Two-Bit Haircut

Coming of age is a delicate and difficult matter for most kids. It was no different for me. Desires of the mind precede the growth of the body. The urge to drive a car hit me long before I could get my beginner's license. The desperation of wanting to be with the opposite sex by far anticipated the time when my folks thought it was appropriate. Being a kid, with its need to always ask, "Mother, may I?" didn't allow for much creativity. It seemed like everyone else always got to call the shots. Surely adulthood would release me from all those stifling restrictions. Why I had what occurs in a barber shop somehow tied to my future manhood you are about to discover for yourself.

One of the things that I had identified with being grown up was a male's ability to grow facial hair. I was fascinated with the process of Dad's morning shave. Many times I would lather up and pretend to shave my beard with the back side of a comb. Then I would get a washcloth and soak it with as much hot water as I could. I'd dab at my face. Ouch! Why couldn't Dad use cold water instead of hot? It was one of the many mysteries of youth.

When I went to the barber shop, I hated to have the barber get one of those booster seats and put it in the chair. One barber had a board he put across the arms of the chair. And it wasn't even padded, it was just a plain old board, with splinters and all. I mean, it was bad enough being a short kid, but when a booster seat was inserted into the equation, I just knew everyone in the shop was thinking, "Hey, look at the short kid who needs a booster seat. When will he ever grow up?"

Occasionally, I would hear the expression "Shave and a haircut — two bits." I never knew what that meant. I never cared to ask. It wasn't at the top of my list of inquiries. Anyway, by the time I was riding my bike to the barber shop, haircuts were already at the outlandishly inflated price of one dollar. There was one thing I noticed after I outgrew the booster seat. That, in itself, was quite an indication that I was on my way to manhood, not needing the booster seat, I mean. But there was one other matter that seemed to be unfair to us guys who were doing our best to behave as adults. Men always got their ears and the backs of their necks "cleaned" with a safety razor. After the haircut was finished, a final detail of trimming those fine hairs was administered to a man by shaving the neck with a real razor, but never to me.

It seemed the height of discrimination at the time. I gave a lot of thought as to why men got a razor trim but boys didn't. Was our skin too tender? Did it cost extra? Were the barbers shortchanging us, knowing we were too stupid to make an issue of it? Why were we neglected in the monthly administration of the razor? It seemed unfair. It was unfair. But I never had the gall to ask a barber why he wouldn't shave around my neck and ears. Besides, I surely didn't relish the sight of blood.

But one fine day my beloved sire and I were visiting at Campbell Keen's, an old family friend. As was often the case, I needed a haircut badly. Campbell told my father that a retired barber lived down the street and gave great haircuts. And on top of that, he only charged a quarter. Down to his basement shop we headed. It was the best haircut of my life, bar none. The old barber didn't even hint of a booster seat, though I was at that size when it could have gone either way. He talked to me just like I was a grown up. He seemed to genuinely care about what I thought of the matters we discussed. And after my haircut was finished, he did the nicest thing that had ever been done to me in my life in a barber's chair. Oh, I had had barbers put on those hand held vibrators and rub my shoulders and neck. But I always thought that it was a sign of a poor barber, one who couldn't cut hair all that well and had to add something extra to keep his customers. Although I have to admit, I did enjoy the neck massage much better than the haircut itself. And some would give me suckers, which also gave me mixed emotions. I mean, I wanted the sucker, but I also wanted to be treated like a man, and men weren't offered suckers, at least not very often. Some barbers gave baseball cards or a free haircut, after you paid for the first ten cuts, of course.

Just guess what this old barber did for me? That's right. He shaved around my ears and neck. He didn't ask if I'd like a shave. He didn't ask my father if it was okay. He just grabbed that straight razor and began to slap it back and forth on the old razor strap. It was music to my ears. He lathered me up and started the ritual that all young men must experience before properly attaining manhood. What a thrill it was. The warmth of the hot shaving cream against my skin felt terrific. The steel of the blade gliding skillfully across my skin was a new sensation entirely. Wow! "So this is what it feels like being a man." I had arrived.

One thing Dad was always sensitive about when I got a haircut was that I was allowed to pay the barber myself, just like it was really my money. That always felt good. So I had a crisp dollar bill at hand for those moments when I suavely asked, "Well, how much do I owe you?" So, in the most grown-up voice I could muster, for I felt more grown up then than ever before, I asked, "Well, sir, how much do I owe you?" His reply took me off guard and reminded me suddenly of just how ungrown up I really was. "That'll be two bits, Sonny Boy!" I was speechless. Not only did I not know how much two bits was, which indicated how unworldly wise I was, but I felt like a kid again after he called me "Sonny" and "Boy" all in the same breath. My Dad came to my immediate rescue and said, "Two bits is a quarter, Stevie. So just give him the dollar and he'll give you change for the difference."

I gave the barber my dollar bill and awaited change. "How can this poor old fellow make any money if all he charges is a quarter?" I thought to myself. He gave me back three quarters in change. Being sensitive to the man's generosity in charging me so little, I tipped him another two bits. It was the only time I can recall tipping a barber 100%. It felt good. He was delighted with my thoughtfulness and I went on my way rejoicing.

Haircuts are not one of my favorite things. But, all in all, that was probably the most memorable time I ever experienced in a barber's chair. Well, there was that time when I gave my typical "a little off the sides and back" and ended up with the worst butcher job I have ever seem performed on a human's scalp. After that episode I never went back to a barber school again for a cheap haircut. But that's also another story. Now, if I could only find a barber who could take a little off the back and somehow transplant it to the front. Sigh! Manhood!!

"Time to Come Home!"

The sound of Mom or Dad calling me home when I was a kid was music to my ears. Most of my playmates hated it when they were called home and had to interrupt important matters such as cowboys and Indians or "Ketch." Whether my parents called on the phone or stood on the porch and yelled in the general direction toward where I was playing at the time, the call meant supper was ready or it was getting too dark and I needed to head toward the house. One of the greatest blessings of life, though I wasn't fully aware of it at the time, was being able to grow up in a Christian home where there were rules of conduct and chores to be done and accountability for infractions. Home was a safe haven where the Goad kids could eat and sleep and be nurtured without giving it a second thought.

Thomas Wolfe has more or less given us the notion that we just can't go home again, that visions of the past we attempt to make contact with years later simply are no longer touchable. It is postulated that they have vanished into the nebulous marching of time and the altering of our space and matter, sort of like putting your hand into a swift moving river and pulling it out and then trying to put your hand back into that same river again. It can't be done. The river has moved on and will never be the same again.

One fond memory of my childhood is Grandma Goad's farmhouse in Kentucky. It surely wasn't a showpiece by today's standards, but it had all the ingredients a city kid needed to make life more interesting than it was back in the "modern world." Going to Grandma's was like stepping back in history. There were feather beds that seemed to literally swallow you up at night. There were the smells of the kerosene lamps and wood burning in the stove and chicken frying on the stove and the farm animal aromas all around. It was full of neat places to explore, like the cellar where we all went during bad thunderstorms, lined with shelves of Grandma Goad's homemade preserves. There was the cistern for collecting water for bathing and clothes-washing. There were the well and the holler and the woodpile. Between two buildings was a large oak tree where we learned to do some serious climbing. There was no running water and no electricity. The outhouse was the least appreciated place of all, that is, until a kid decided he couldn't contain himself for the entire weekend's visit.

Years into my adulthood I made a pilgrimage back to that old homestead of my youth, where the sounds of Grandma and Grandpa and Great Aunt Avy echoed busily in my childhood ears. Boards had been placed over the well. The cisterns had disappeared. The sounds of pigs and hens and cows could no longer be heard. Someone had stored grain, waist high, right smack dab in the middle of the living room of the farmhouse. The place was a mere skeleton of what I remembered from my youth. The only thing that looked almost as it had when I was a kid was the old oak tree. It stood in its place like a giant sentinel overlooking the passages of time. As I sadly stood at the same place where many childhood memories held such sway, Wolfe's last novel seemed to be speaking to me out loud: "You can't go home again, Stevie." What I was attempting to do was the sentiment expressed by the author in his first novel "Look Homeward, Angel."

But perhaps Wolfe was right. Maybe we can't go back and relive the past. Perhaps we ought not dare to try. Because, after all, "the past is prologue" as the Bard himself might say. Every time I visit my old haunts in Indiana I am reminded of that truth. They are never as I have remembered them. The high school I attended seems altogether different. And it is. The students are not the same. The environs have aged. When I visit old home places they have revealed a mere glimpse of the past, but not much else. Even when I look up old school chums, they are not the ones I knew long ago. They are different people, with different faces and different outlooks on life. Some of them have grown to be so surprisingly different from myself that in the embarrassment of small talk we blush at how little we now have in common. I tried to look up a teacher or two and discovered some of my favorites had already given up their spirits to eternity.

So, with a sigh of resignation, I almost give in to young Master Wolfe's decree about the past. Things do change. People do grow in different directions. Houses wear out and the infrastructures of cities rise and wane like waves of the sea. The cityscape I recall of Indianapolis has changed so dramatically that if it weren't for Monument Circle I could hardly distinguish it from any other modern metropolis in the land. The RCA/Hoosier Dome and Market Square Arena and the Convention Center and the athletic venues available at Indiana University/Purdue University Indianapolis make the skyline of that great midwestern city almost a stranger to me. These places were only images in the minds of visionaries as I was being reared there.

Ah, but that is the point, isn't it? Vision! Whether forward, as the planners of today's Circle City envisioned a metropolis on the cutting edge of modern society with all of the cultural and social avenues open to such a locale, or backward, to a simpler time where the buildings barely even hinted of touching the sky and the steel of electric streetcar tracks could still be seen peeping out of the middle of the asphalt, I can have both cities any time I want to visit them. The Indianapolis of 1949, where I walked the sidewalks of Washington Street hand in hand with my father and witnessed an occasional horse-drawn wagon making its trek to who knows where, that city is mine for the visiting, so long as I have its vision in my memory. I can visit the modern city any time I go back to see my father or my sister or my "hometown." But visiting my boyhood homes and favorite teachers and best playmates and most memorable events can all be done without purchasing an airline ticket or budgeting so much money for gas and hotel accommodations on the way. I can visit 3117 East Bradbury Street or 3117 East Wade Street or the Fountain Square Church of Christ or Bean Creek or Margaret McFarland Public School #4 or Bosma's Dairy Bar in Beech Grove or Tacoma's onion fields or Mr. Smithson's strawberry patches or ride my bike to Garfield Park; I can visit these places any day and any time, in my memory. As long as God allows me to have a preacher's "ready recollection," I can instantly recall the days of my youth before the evil days drew near and relive them as though they only happened yesterday.

Maybe I can challenge Wolfe's premise. "Thomas, you can go home again!" I've done it a hundred times and more. I do it every time I write a story of my past. Memories. How marvelous they are. Painful ones. Solemn ones. Hurtful ones and happy ones. Memories of kith and kin, of puppy loves and heartbreaks, of long departed loved ones, of moments that are not constrained by the passing of time and the revolving of planets. Yes! I can go home again, and I will. "Precious memories, how they linger. How they ever flood my soul."

Out of Loneliness

Oh, to have enough friends and family and neighbors and associates to be able to enjoy the luxury of choosing to be alone as often as possible. For, it is in the having of loved ones that allows time alone to be profitable and meaningful. For those who genuinely are alone, not because they have decided to go off by themselves to a quiet place to meditate, but for whatever reasons find themselves without a support team who cares, suicide is often the option. Or, maybe other forms of escape not so immediately terminal are tried: booze, drugs, sex, gambling, etc. For, loneliness, and being alone, are two separate things.

I was alone for several years. Oh, I had acquaintances and friends. Church family gave me holy hugs from time to time. But for seven years I was alone, by myself, wandering in the desert of self-pity on occasion, wondering where I might find solace. At first being alone was enjoyable. I had always liked being by myself under certain circumstances. Being gregarious and finding it easy to make friends, people who know me well might find that hard to believe. I reveled in the blessing of being able to go off to write or read or pray or simply to listen to nature. It was cleansing. I recall that in earlier times on some occasions at family gatherings when the decibel level got too much for me, I would quietly slip off by myself and hardly be missed. Those were times when I chose to be alone. Loneliness is another matter entirely.

For seven years of my adult life I was not only alone, but I was also lonely. I had no one to cry with and no one to laugh with and found myself at mid-life wondering where I was headed. Being alone is manageable. Being lonely is heartbreaking. None of God's creatures ought to have to be lonely. Some people are lonely because they have treated others so shabbily and have been so self-centered that they have driven away all those who would have been close by. That becomes a matter of reaping what we sow. I was an individual who could never have too many friends. There was always room for one more. Thus, my loneliness was not a matter of not having friends. It wasn't even a matter of being ignored by associates. It was a loneliness that God used, like a crucible, to refine my character and to make me a better person. It was a loneliness of the soul. Perhaps the worst kind of loneliness.

We all realize that one can be in a crowd of people, even be the center of attention in a crowd, and still be lonely. One doesn't have to be alone to be lonely. Loneliness has nothing to do with how many people are in close proximity. It has to do with how we relate to those around us. I much prefer being alone on occasion than being lonely. Being alone is a choice. It is even a good choice that finds its support in Scripture. Being lonely is not a choice. It just happens to us. It envelops us slowly, almost imperceptibly, until one day we realize we have become captive to this state of being detached from others in the most negative way possible.

Being alone often afforded me time for meditation and introspection. Some people are so harried, because of commitments, that they haven't time to simply meditate. Getting in that mode is a mistake so far as I am concerned. Being lonely reminded me that life can be an emotional roller coaster that thrusts us into moments of pain that we would like to avoid if we had a choice about it. My loneliness was good for me, almost therapeutic. It forced me to take inventory of my life. It made me separate the significant from the mundane. It allowed me to develop a sensitivity for others that I hadn't yet learned to offer. Loneliness made me more grateful for the little things in life, for the simple expressions of affection. It afforded me a framework from which to be more sympathetic to those with mental and emotional problems themselves.

During my lonely years, I wrote more letters to old friends than I ever had before. Instead of wallowing in woe-is-me navel gazing, I made contact with family. My sons were on my mind. My father was visited more frequently. Loneliness is hard to define, because as I reflect on it now, I wasn't lonely because I didn't have those who cared for me. I wasn't lonely because I couldn't find someone to be with. Perhaps I was lonely because God wanted me to understand how depressed and desperate souls can actually become.

During my lonely period I visited a large and active church. It had a formal singles ministry. I was there attempting to connect, not with a partner, but with people who may have been in the same predicament in which I found myself. There was a speaker at one of the singles meetings who had just written a book about being single again. He mentioned ten of the most life-sapping experiences that could befall an individual. These were the kinds of things that would drive people to drink, or suicide. Each tragedy had so many numerical points of value assigned to it. If one had a certain number of total points, it meant they were prime candidates for mental collapse, or so-called, nervous breakdown. As I recall, the score that indicated one had crossed over into the danger zone was about 300. My score was over 600. Thus, I was supposed to be an emotional cripple. By all standards I should have been a total emotional wreck. I suppose, in some ways, I was crippled, for my very presence at such a singles gathering indicated that I was seeking help, lest I drown in my own loneliness.

After that meeting, I focused on what factors in my life might be contributing to my forlorn state. That meeting with the author told me something I had never put down in thought, let alone put down on paper. Within one year's time, I had experienced the collapse of my marriage, the loss of my job, a life threatening illness and financial devastation. The only constant during that period was my relationship with God. I never thought one time of cursing him and quitting my involvement in church and spiritual matters. I never stopped teaching and sharing my faith with others. So, the big question that is forced to the front is this: How can one be close to God and still experience loneliness? Perhaps I don't have a good answer for that, but I know that even God was lonely. For it was Jesus Himself who said on the cross, "My God, my God, why have you forsaken me?"

Loneliness isn't often a permanent illness. I don't even know if it is an illness. It sure felt like it at the time. I am no longer lonely. But being there drew me closer to my God. Being there caused me to appreciate my Savior all the more. Circumstances can cause us to experience emotional upheavals that are almost unexplainable, even inexplicable. In my loneliness, I never gave up on God. I never thought He forsook me. I never forsook Him.

Deliverance is a beautiful thing. I now can feel sensations I never before understood. One has to shovel a lot of snow in order to genuinely appreciate the heat of the desert southwest. One has to be sick on occasion to fully comprehend how precious and meaningful health really is. Poverty has allowed a lot of us to appreciate more significantly those times when cash flow isn't a problem. So, my years of loneliness, though surrounded by many loving people who truly cared for my soul, taught me to listen more closely, sympathize more eagerly, express my thankfulness more openly and offer my love less selfishly.

Loneliness can cause us to be deceived. It can make us think we *are* alone. Maybe people will not, at times, fill that loneliness void, but He is always there. Perhaps the various activities in which we engage ourselves do not satisfy the longing for closeness and intimacy with another human being, but our Lord has promised to never forsake us or leave us. Believe it.

Chapter Eight

Imaginary Journeys

D'jever?

As a young boy back in Indiana, we had some ways of getting right to the point. We made use of several linguistic shortcuts at our disposal. Most folk refer to them as contractions. Most everyone uses them from time to time. Like saying "can't" for "cannot" to save one syllable. And we often use "you're" instead of "you are" or "it's" in place of "it is."

But this doesn't quite catch the flavor of some of our contractions. We actually used to see how many words we could cram into one. My favorite is "smatter." It replaces four distinct words. "What is the matter?" "Smatter, Fred? You look awfully sad." The word I use for this article is like this. It is a substitute for saying, "Did you ever?" Sort of like Andy Rooney beginning one of his harangues with "D'jever wonder why such and such always happens?"

With this intro in mind, let me ask all of us a few "D'jevers." D'jever wonder why people who claim to love the Lord with all their hearts can barely roll out for church services once or twice a month? D'jever wonder why people who always come to the church for help when they are down and out seldom support it financially when they are "up and in"? D'jever wonder why the biggest complainers at church are usually the ones who do the least? It's amazing how becoming involved causes people to focus more on what can be done, rather than on what is wrong.

D'jever wonder why a godly man whose name is proposed as elder can be cannibalized by brethren for some error or weakness he had decades earlier? D'jever wonder who ends up doing all that work that just seems to get done by itself when nobody ever volunteered to do it in the first place? D'jever wonder how one busy disciple can get more done in half the time than a committee that is appointed to look into it? D'jever wonder why some people who call themselves Christians can never find the time to confess Jesus to neighbors and friends? D'jever ask God for something purely unselfish and find Him giving it to you almost immediately; and then think "wasn't that a coincidence?"

D'jever wonder how Christians who give ten percent and more of their income can live so much better than those who are selfish with their money? D'jever notice how easy it is for some people to find Scripture in their Bibles and then wonder how they are able to do that? D'jever think how sad this old world would be without the love and joy that disciples of Christ spread on a daily basis? D'jever wonder how a so-called atheist can say the universe has no designer, but something far less complex, like his car, had to have a designer? D'jever discover during a fresh morning sunrise, or a colorful evening sunset, the magnanimous presence of God and found yourself thrilled at knowing of His merciful grace in Jesus?

D'jever imagine what this world would be like if there were no churches or Bibles or babies? D'jever think of how hopeless we would be if it were not for the Word of God revealing our origins and destinations? D'jever forget to thank

God for your spleen? When was the last time you did? We find it easier to thank Him for our health and our food, shelter and clothing, but until your spleen fails you, it's not on your mind much, is it? D'jever find the bed so comforting and restful that you forgot to say your evening prayers? D'jever think so little of your mate and children that you forgot to tell them how much you love them? D'jever find yourself so glued to the TV that you mistreated your family by shouting at them? D'jever think of how wonderful heaven will be?

D'jever find yourself taking God's grace and love for granted on a daily basis?

D'jever? I sure have!

Salt of the Earth

In one way or another, we are supposed to be the salt of the earth. Christians are not only to add flavor to their world, but are also to be the light of the world. Without disciples of Christ seasoning and lighting their environments, the world will continue to decay and to degenerate into an abysmal cauldron of rottenness and depravity. Instead of being conformed to the world, we are to transform our minds and thus facilitate the conformation of the world into the image of Jesus. It isn't an easy task. Nobody said it would be. But it is a doable task. This is the story of one fellowship of Christians that rose to the challenges of Christ and of Paul.

One church in a small town had been doing things, more or less, the way that had always been done for years. They met at the typical times for Bible class and worship assembly. They even had a Sunday evening worship service, without anyone questioning why a repeat assembly was necessary. They met for midweek Bible study on the orthodox day of meeting, namely, Wednesday. During the summer, when Bible class teachers desperately needed some relief, the church would conduct what it called, because others called it this, Vacation Bible School. Rather than having some needed time off, the teachers were taxed even further to teach classes every night for two weeks in a row.

Occasionally, in classes, a token reading of what Christians call, "The Great Commission," was heard. It is that marvelous passage where Jesus tells disciples to disciple others, baptize them and then teach them all the things He had taught. But little of this seemed to be getting done in this particular fellowship. The group had actually diminished in size over a period of a decade, yet the community in which it was located had doubled in number. All the earmarks that are generally looked to as growth signs were subtly whispering that the church was dying. There were fewer baptisms each year. The contribution had flattened out and was even beginning to slip somewhat. The attendance figures were the real telltale sign. Attendance was off by some forty percent.

It is a tragedy to have to admit it, but some of our traditions have become sacred cows to us. If they are challenged by anyone, sides are usually chosen and the friction ensues. Anyone who asks, "Why are we doing this when it obviously isn't accomplishing what we are hoping for?" is suspect. Let some new and innovative strategies for outreach be introduced, especially by a new parson in town, and they are challenged and rejected, as if *methods*, in and of themselves, were anathema to God. We have parroted for years the notion of generic commandments, one of which is the commission to evangelize our world, but when new generic ways of doing just that are promoted, there is blood to pay for attempting to change the "old paths" as they are sometimes called.

Speaking of old paths, when I visited Grandpa Goad's farm, there was a path that led to the outhouse. It was an old path, too. It was oft traveled. I hated to take it. But it was the only path available. It was one of the things I disliked most about visiting the farm. Most of my life I had enjoyed inside plumbing. I was a city slicker. Sitting in a dark shed with spiders and other creepy crawlers wasn't the way I had learned to enjoy those intimate moments by myself in the water closet. I had even heard that some people kicked against the idea of inside toilets at first. "Inside? Inside the house?!" They couldn't imagine such an arrangement. But, folks, it's so much better inside. It may have been a new idea. It surely was innovative. But, it was also better.

Remember the story about the girl who was cooking for her new husband for the first time? She took a pot roast and cut off one end of it and put it in a pan. Her husband asked why she cut off so much of the roast. She explained that it was how her mother had taught her and that she didn't know why. So, she called her mother and asked why she had always cut the end off the pot roast. Her mother said it was how Grandma had taught her. So she called Grandma and asked about the tradition of cutting off a large portion of the roast. Grandma explained, "Honey, I cut off the end of the roast because my pot was just too small."

We engage in programs and ministries in much the same

way today. We meet at times set down years ago by our grandparents in the faith. We conduct what we call "gospel meetings" and see few results. They are throwbacks to the old brush arbor meetings of yore, where large crowds once sat spellbound for hours as some orator broke the bread of life. But, of course, that was in the years B.T. (Before Television). We have visitation programs that do little but get a few people, out of guilt, to come out on Tuesday evenings and call on the few who are sick, or those who have recently visited the church services. And the church continues to decline. And we wonder why.

Back to my story. The church that was declining hired a new cheerleader, that is, full time paid gospel preacher (often called senior minister, or evangelist, or pulpit minister). This particular minister had a gift, a gift that had often been looked upon with suspicion and disdain by former church leaders where he had previously labored. He had even been dismissed from one congregation for being so "liberal" as they put it. In spite of this occasional challenge to his ideas, the new preacher arrived in town with high hopes of finding a church with open-minded leaders. In the "tryout" and interviews, he was told that the church wanted an aggressive and energetic evangelist who would inspire the church to become more evangelistic, like the early church. He informed the leaders that this was just the kind of fellowship he was hoping to find and that he would help them do just that, if they would let him.

At their first official meeting together, when Brother "Jones" presented his first wave of ideas to the church leaders, they were dumbfounded. A few of the leaders were even agitated and fearful. What Parson Jones had done was to call them immediately to task on their stated pledge to be more evangelistic. He outlined various methods, some proven and some not proven, but all surprisingly interesting. He asked the church to give reasons for the programs that were already in place. He asked everyone to help analyze whether the old programs were accomplishing what they were intended to accomplish. After all, methods shouldn't be etched in stone.

This church actually had two signs in front of the building with the times of its services literally etched in stone. They were sandstone signs. As might be expected, the only thing that wasn't etched in stone was, of course, the preacher's name. It's hard to chisel out the name of a new preacher every year or two. Anyway, some began to undermine the work of this new preacher immediately. But, amazingly, most of the leaders seemed eager to take a chance with new methods that seemed thoughtful and logical. They realized that methodology wasn't necessarily conservative or liberal, that it was more "neutral" than anything else. The leaders agreed that they were tired of the status quo and the lack of growth. So, with much prayer, they set about to implement some of the new strategies outlined by Parson Jones.

Over the next three years, many of the old and ineffective programs, that had been intended for outreach, were scrapped. The financially draining bus program, that had been in effect for over a decade, was scuttled. It was pointed out that there were over 200 half empty "buses" every Sunday sitting in the parking lot during worship assembly. There hadn't been a need for buses in the first place. The few who were brought on buses could have just as easily been brought to church in the members' automobiles. Vacation Bible School was discontinued and in its place was put an organized system of teaching for the Sunday School program that took children through the entire Bible every three years. In other words, there would be Vacation Bible School taught every Sunday of the year.

One diametric change that was begun, with much grumbling and complaining by the old guard who thought the very boundaries of Christianity itself were being tampered with, was in regard to the official times of meeting. Instead of 9:30 a.m. Sunday School and 10:30 a.m. Worship, the assembly time was changed to 2:30 in the afternoon, with the Bible classes following. This move alone caused the attendance to almost double in one year. Why? Because all those people we invite to church, who attend other churches, couldn't come without missing their own assemblies. There was no Sunday evening assembly. Why? Because the service had already been held that day, and there seemed no reasonable explanation for why the traditional evening service should be perpetuated. Whatever factors led to evening service on Sunday, whether it was to accommodate farmers or shift workers, those factors were no longer material to their particularly unique local situation.

Instead of simply discarding the evening service, an assembly service was begun on Tuesday evenings which was geared to evangelism. Members were encouraged to bring their neighbors, relatives, friends and others to this assembly. The sermons were soul-inviting messages, not typical homilies that are often themes of moral excellence that could be taught in any church or synagogue in the land. The Wednesday evening Bible study was changed to Thursday evening. This was promoted in the local media and many people from various churches began attending. The genius of having Thursday evening open Bible studies was that most other churches had Wednesday evening classes or prayer meetings. With the new meeting schedule, there was no conflict.

One other thing that was done, which, when you think about it for a minute was not all that profound, was the encouragement of members to visit in the other churches. Christians were told to "infiltrate" the classes and assemblies of other churches and challenge error when it was taught, to challenge it in a loving and friendly manner, but to challenge it nonetheless. Some of the members actually became Bible class teachers and were allowed to teach in the educational programs of the other churches, since many of those churches were short of teachers. This alone reached many souls and taught them the word of God more perfectly.

As you might guess, this suggestion of going to other churches and incorporating into their fellowships, was met with much initial disapproval. All the old bromides were offered. "It can't be done. It's never been done like that before. We will lose our members to the other churches. What if someone accepts something we don't believe?" What the disbelievers forgot was that truth need not fear confrontation. Truth is only enhanced when it is inspected more closely. So, with the providence of God abounding, the leaders of the church carefully and fearlessly responded to the challenges presented them, and the church grew. It grew because of the new spirit of fellowship. Instead of holding services and preaching to themselves, the church began to do what Jesus asked all Christians to do, to reach out to others in the spirit of brotherly love and with no motive in mind but to share the precious gospel of Jesus with others.

After three years of dispensing with old methods, introducing some new ones, and modifying existing programs, the church took on a new image and personality. The attendance more than tripled and the baptisms quadrupled. Not only was the church now obeying the mandate of Christ to disciple souls as they went out into their world, but it was experiencing the marvelous product of the Lord's promise: "And I will give the increase."

No, you can't visit this particular congregation of God's people. Because, you see, it doesn't really exist, except in my mind. And the reason it doesn't exist is because we are all people of closed minds, whether we admit it or not. We easily suspect. We are not easily changed. New methodologies are terrifying to those of us who are at ease in Zion. And if there were a congregation with just this recent history and present profile, you wouldn't need to visit it anyway, because the things that work for it might not be the best methods that would work where you are. It is amazing how church leaders, fearful of their churches dying, or worse, afraid of becoming irrelevant, will visit Willow Creek and other evangelical churches that are experiencing phenomenal growth and then go home and try to copy what they saw. And they wonder why it doesn't work back home.

Friends, whether it is suburban Chicago or the corner of 8th and Plumb in Possum Trot, Idaho, there is only one formula for being the family of God or a disciple of Christ. The formula is as old as the gospel itself. And one doesn't need to buy a best-seller by Elmer Towns on church growth to discover it. One doesn't need to visit all the mega and meta churches in the land. Rather, one must be willing to begin the change within himself. He must be willing to go to his prayer closet and ask God for direction and power. And then, he must open the pages of his dusty Bible and read. A good place to begin would be Matthew 28:18 straight through to the end of the book of Acts.

I went to the doctor and told him that when I held my hand "this" way it hurt. The doctor replied, "Don't hold your hand that way." The church needs to go to the Great Physician and have a checkup. In many areas of the world the church is hurting, too. But the pain is caused by our own posture, a posture of elitism and partisanship and sectarianism and exclusivism. And the Lord is displeased. Is He attempting to tell us, "Quit holding your hand that way"? Is He saying, "Stop holding services that way"? Interestingly, the term "worship service" isn't found in all of Scripture.

Salt doesn't do its best in a salt shaker. Light doesn't do its job while hidden under a basket. Are we simply not listening? When He comes to find fruit and sees us withered and dead, will He say, "Cut it down! Why is it taking up space?" God, forbid!

"Pickles and Extra Onions, Only"

How some of those fast food chains got to be so big is beyond understanding. It's one of those all time great mysteries of modern civilization. I mean, have you ever got an order exactly correct, especially at a drive-thru window? Sure, if you order a large ice tea, they might get that right. But if you have anything more than what is standard fare, forget it. I lost count of the times I have ordered a small black coffee for my wife and been asked, "Would you like cream and sugar with that black coffee?"

One of them: "Welcome to Fricasseed Froglegs! May I help you?"

Me: "I'd like a hamburger with pickles and extra onions, only, please, and a large Coke."

Them: "Can you repeat that, please?"

Me: "I said, I'd like a hamburger with pickles and extra onions, only, and a large Coke."

Them: "Okay. That's a hamburger with extra pickles and onions, and a large Coke. Right?"

Me: "That's close. I want a hamburger with pickles and extra onions, only, and a large Coke."

Them: "That's what I said."

Me: "No it isn't! You said 'extra pickles and onions.' I said, 'pickles and extra onions.' I don't want extra pickles. I only want extra onions!"

Them: "Sorry. Okay, you want a hamburger with extra onions and nothing else, right?"

Me: "No! I want a hamburger with pickles. Got that? Pickles and extra onions! Extra onions!! Got that?"

Them: "Yes, sir. You want a hamburger with pickles and extra onions, right?"

Me: "Exactamundo, señor."

Them: "Would you like something to drink with that?"

Me: "Of course. I already told you I wanted a large Coke."

You see, I know how the system works. I once managed a hamburger joint. It was a big chain store. I worked for the home office and managed a company training store. We trained managers and franchise owners to operate our stores. It was at a time when we had 500 stores and McDonalds only had 300. We had an edge on the competition, open flame-broiled burgers. And it was fun. Sort of. One thing I learned that has helped me through the years, but has also caused me to want to commit "hari-kari" a few times: Never order what is typical menu food. Order something a little different. If they put catsup and mustard on their Super Duper Burger, order it without catsup. That way they can't give you one of those burgers that might have been in a holding bin for a few months. They have to do a "grill" and make you a fresh one.

Well, over the years, I have rarely ordered just what is on the menu, mainly because I don't like my condiments all mixed together like they do it. I mean, who wants mustard, catsup, special sauce and mayonnaise all oozing together and dropping out of the side of a burger you are trying to eat while driving eighty miles an hour down the highway? So, not liking catsup or mustard anyway, and hating mayonnaise altogether, I always order my burgers the old-fashioned way my pappy used to fix 'em, with pickles and extra onions, only.

Them: "Would you like cheese on your hamburger, sir?"

Me: (By now I am getting somewhat annoyed at the lack of training of this employee). "No, if I wanted cheese on my hamburger I would have ordered a cheeseburger, wouldn't I?"

Them: "No need to get testy!"

Me: "Look, all I want is a simple hamburger. Just a plain old simple burger like I have asked for, over and over. Now can you please just do it?"

Them: "You want your hamburger plain? I thought you said you wanted pickles and onions."

Me: "I do want pickles and onions!"

Them: "Then why did you say, 'Plain'?"

Me: "Look, I'm tired of this hassle. Is your manager there?"

Them: "Speaking."

Me: "You're the manager? You've got to be kidding. Why can't you get my order right the first time around? I go through this all the time with you guys. Read my lips. I want a hamburger with pickles and extra onions. That's it. Zip. Nothing else. Got it?"

Them: "You mean you don't want your large Coke?"

Me: "Father, forgive them, for they know not what they do."

Them: "What was that?"

Me: "Yes!"

Them: "Yes, what?"

Me: "Okay. Yes, please."

Them: "No! I mean, do you still want that Coke?"

Me: "Yes! Yes!! Yes!!! I want the Cooooooooke!!!!"

Them: "Would you like light or heavy ice?"

Me: "I thought all ice weighed pretty much the same."

Them: "No. I mean, do you want lots of ice or little ice?"

Me: "Medium."

Them: "Sorry, sir. We can't cook our hamburgers medium anymore. FDA rules and all, you know."

Me: "No! No!! No!!! I want medium ice!!!!"

Them: "But I thought you said you wanted a *large* Coke."

Me: "Is this Lou Costello?"

Them: "I beg your pardon?"

Me: "Forget it. I want a large Coke with medium ice! *Medium ice in the large Coke!! Got it?!!*"

Them: "No need to yell, sir. I can hear you just fine."

Me: "Sorry. I guess I lost it there for a minute."

Them: "If you drive up to the second window, that'll be $27.59."

I have always wondered how much the bill would be if I went to the first window. I mean, why have two windows when they only use the second one? Is that first window for VIP's or what? Does anyone actually work that first window? Is it a job like the coal stoker on a Diesel locomotive? Does someone get paid for just sitting there by the window?

Them: "Here's your order, sir."

Me: "Thanks."

Never, never, ever drive away from a drive-thru window without first checking your order. I've lost count of the times I got home only to find the food not remotely resembling what I had ordered, or else it was sorta like I ordered, only with the mayonnaise oleo oozing out of a wet bun. So, here I sit checking my order. Humm. Let me see if they got it right for a change. Nope. This is a fish fillet sandwich with a small root beer! Why me, Lord? What have I ever done?

Me: Honk! Tap on window. "Hey, is anyone in there?"

Them: "May I help you?"

Me: "Where's the manager who just took this order?"

Them: "What order?"

Me: "Oh, I can see he has trained you well."

Them: "What do you mean?"

Me: "Never mind. This is the wrong order. This is a fish sandwich and a root beer. I ordered a hamburger and Coke."

Them: "Sorry about that. What did you want on your hamburger?"

Me: "Oh, the usual. And give me a large drink, too. You decide. I'm sort of in a hurry. I had to be at the doctor's office an hour ago to have him check me and see why I have ulcers and colon problems. He thinks it might have something to do with my diet."

Them: "Hey, Mister, it's your lucky day. I happen to have a hamburger here, with pickles and extra onions and a large Coke. Some inconsiderate jerk drove off and stiffed us for the order. Can you believe the gall some people have?"

Me: "Yeah, I know what you mean!"

Inconvenient?

A young pregnant mother is sitting in an examining room at her doctor's clinic. The conversation unfolds as she fumbles with a milk bottle while feeding her one-year-old son. She begins with these words: "Doctor, I have something very serious to talk to you about."

Doctor: "Are you feeling sick?"

Mother: "No. It's not about me. Well, I guess it is about me, but, I mean, I need to ask you to do me a favor."

Doctor: "What kind of favor?

Mother: "I've decided I want to terminate my pregnancy. I'm too young to have two babies. I don't have a husband and I just won't be able to make it if I have another child."

Doctor: "Remember when you asked me for birth control advice? Remember when I advised you not to engage in sexual relations before marriage? Remember the high price I said might be paid for such behavior?"

Mother: "Yes, I remember. But, my boyfriend said he loved me and that if I loved him I should go all the way with him."

Doctor: "Where is he today?"

Mother: "I have no idea. He deserted me the minute he found out I was pregnant."

Doctor: "Is he the father of this child you are carrying?"

Mother: "No. I found a new boyfriend."

Doctor: "Are you going to marry him?"

Mother: "No, he left, too. I mean, he said he wasn't mature enough to become a father and have all that responsibility. You know?"

Doctor: "Yes, I know. I know very well. I know that too many girls like you get pregnant and then want me to help make the problem go away. And, I must confess, I don't like to be in that kind of position."

Mother: "But aren't you supposed to help people with their medical problems? I find this pregnancy to be very inconvenient."

Doctor: "Inconvenient? I'm sure it is an inconvenience to have to raise two children at such a young age, and without the help of a mate. So, what is it you want me to do?"

Mother: "I was in hopes you could do the pregnancy termination for me, since you have been my family physician and all, all these years."

Doctor: "You want me to kill the baby that you are carrying inside of you?"

Mother: "Well, I don't think of it like that. A friend told me that interrupting a pregnancy isn't really killing. It's sort of like getting rid of unwanted fetal tissue."

Doctor: "Do you realize that this 'unwanted fetal tissue,' as you call it, already has its sex determined? That it has a heartbeat and digestive system and fingernails and lungs, and that it is already a miniature person?"

Mother: "I was told that a fetus isn't a person; that it is merely a mass of cells."

Doctor: "Those who want to kill little defenseless babies in the womb use terms like 'mass of cells' and 'termination of pregnancy' so they don't have to say what it really is. In reality, that mass of cells is an individual person, a little boy or little girl. And a 'termination of pregnancy" is the killing of that little boy or little girl. Are you sure you have thought through all of this? Has anyone explained the adoption options open to you?"

Mother: "I don't want to go through all of the hassle of filling out papers and wondering about who might get my baby. Besides, I find all of that interviewing and stuff stressful."

Doctor: "Have you considered the stress we will be putting on your little unborn child if we take its life? What about the inconvenience we will be causing him or her?"

Mother: "Look, I just want to get this abortion over with. I don't think you have the right to lecture me on the choice I have made. This is a personal decision and nobody is going to stop me. So, if you won't help me, I'll go to someone who will."

Doctor: "All right. If you have your heart set on this, I suppose there is little I can do. So, I guess I will terminate the life of your child for you."

Mother: "Thank you so much, doctor. I knew I could depend on you."

Doctor: "What is your son's name?"

Mother: "I beg your pardon."

Doctor: "If I am going to take the life of a child, I surely want to know his name."

Mother: "I don't know if it's a boy or a girl. I haven't even considered giving it a name because I am going to get rid, I mean, terminate my pregnancy."

Doctor: "I am asking for the name of your present son, your one-year-old."

Mother: "Why do you need his name, doctor?"

Doctor: "I need his name for my records so that after we 'terminate' him, we can keep a file for legal reasons and all. It's not every day a woman comes into my office and asks me to kill her child for her."

Woman: "Now wait just a damn minute here! You're not going to kill my son. I want my other child killed! I mean, I want to have an abortion! You know what I want!!"

Doctor: "Yes, ma'am. I know what you want. You are inconvenienced by having to have children at an early age. It's a hassle to have to mother and love a life you have chosen to bring into the world. So, I just thought I'd make life a lot more convenient for you by killing your present child instead of the one you are carrying. That will give you the added convenience of some free time until the new one arrives, so you can get things together and maybe have some time for yourself. I mean, what difference does it make? Either way I would be terminating a life, right?"

Woman: "What kind of a monster are you? You're crazy, man!"

Doctor: "I don't think so. Why is it okay to kill a baby in the womb, but wrong to kill one outside the womb? Actually, life is precious from the moment of conception. When I became a doctor, I took an oath that began with the words: 'First, do no harm.' I have tried to live up to that oath all my practicing life. I think you understand me clearly. I do not intend to betray that commitment now."

The husbandless mother left hurriedly with her young son riding precariously on her hip. As she slammed the door, she mumbled these words to herself: "You sure can't depend on doctors anymore to help you during a crisis. What is this world coming to?" She walked down the hallway toward the door. As she reached for the door, she paused for just a moment and began to cry. The truth of what her family doctor had told her began to strike a chord in her heart. "Why isn't the life inside of me just as important as the life I'm carrying in my arms now?"

It was a beginning. A window of light began to open. Hopefully, another innocent child will be rescued from the horrors of ungodly choices made by others.

> *"For you created my inmost being;*
> *you knit me together in my*
> *mother's womb.*
> *I praise you because I am fearfully*
> *and wonderfully made;*
> *your works are wonderful,*
> *I know that full well.*
> *My frame was not hidden from you*
> *when I was made in the secret place.*
> *When I was woven together*
> *in the depths of the earth,*
> *your eyes saw my unformed body.*
> *All the days ordained for me were written in your book*
> *before one of them came to be."*

(Psalm 139:13-16, NIV)

Pencil or PC?

Pencils fascinate me. They are such simple writing instruments, yet have accomplished wonders for humanity. Maybe the small things in life are far more important than we are willing to admit.

It seems I have been writing all my life. As I sit at this PC keyboard, it feels like ages ago that I was scribbling my first little essay on school notebook paper, trying to fill in space so the teacher would be pleased. Most of my writing was done with a pencil. Up until recently, it still was. I recall the late and beloved Reuel Lemmons sitting in my study one day writing an editorial for the **Firm Foundation**. He chatted while he wrote. I had envisioned Reuel operating state of the art word processing equipment in order to come up with those magnificent editorials of his. Nope. A yellow pad and a pencil were all he used.

In high school I resisted replacing the pencil with a typewriter. But typing was one of those courses I never regretted. Later, I kicked against changing from a standard to an IBM Selectric. Wow! What a difference! "This has got to be the ultimate in writing. Surely we couldn't improve on the Selectric!" Wrong. Today I sit at my word processor, able to erase mistakes (if I catch them) before they are even on paper. Yet with all of this sophisticated electronic gadgetry at my disposal I still am a pencil sort of guy. Typing is much faster, but something warm is lost in the process. The smell of the wood from sharpening. The ache in my wrist from writer's cramp.

Leonard Read wrote a popular essay years ago titled "I, the Pencil." It pointed out that no one person had the know-how to produce the humble ten-cent writing instrument. And yet it can be manufactured and sold so cheaply. A pencil is merely a length of graphite wrapped by wood. The wood is usually painted some bright color with numbers and words stamped on the outside. Numbers like "2.5" and words like "Have a happy day!" Then there is the rubber eraser bound to one end (unless you are Johnny Carson) by a metal band.

Voilà! The pencil. One can doodle with it or, with its help, change the course of human history. It all depends upon who is holding it at the time.

A pencil is such an economical little package with so much potential. I wrote several evangelistic tracts with one single pencil. Editors have touched hearts and moved nations with their use of the lowly pencil. We used to joke about being so down and out we had to sell pencils on the street corner. I knew a man in Indianapolis who did just that. He sold pencils and other little items out of his coat on Monument Circle. He died wealthy. Selling pencils isn't something to be ashamed of. Nor is the manufacturing of them. I love pencils. I have scads of them at my desk, just in case I am inspired. What, pray tell, would I do with a flash of insight without my little pencil by my tablet, especially during a power outage?

Thank God for little things! Thank God for pencils. Thank God that we have been able to find ways to write down the wonderful news of a dying Savior who rose to guarantee our salvation and eternal life. Next time you are feeling bored, look around. Is there a pencil handy? Pick it up and write to someone who is lonely. Or write to someone who is lost and hopeless. I'd rather have a letter from a friend written in pencil than a signed picture of the President in an envelope sent to "occupant."

The pencil. It may not be as impressive as a 200 Megahertz Pentium computer, with all the bells and whistles, but in a pinch I might just opt for an old yellow number 2. Besides, when I get fidgety, it's a whole lot easier to chew on.

Satan's Board Meeting

"An evil spirit . . . takes with it seven other spirits
more wicked than itself, and they go in and live there"
(Matthew 12:43,45).

Last night I had a horrible dream. It was more like a nightmare. At his headquarters, 666 Sulfur Avenue and Inferno Boulevard, Satan had convened a committee meeting of his wiliest demons to discuss the matter of a great Christian nation in dire need of being influenced for evil. The topic of discussion: "How to demoralize and capture the hearts of the citizens of the United States of America." At the sound of the gavel the discussion commenced.

Satan challenged his gathered henchmen to put their thinking caps on and come up with ideas to tempt and vex the citizenry of the United States, many of whom were putting their trust in Jesus and the Christian life.

"How?" be began. "How are we going to steal these souls away from God?"

He continued, "And how are we going to keep others from putting their faith in Christ?" A hush fell over the usually noisy demons gathered. Finally one senior devil broke the silence with a suggestion.

"Boss," he ventured, "why not try drugs? They've always worked before with other nations."

"Idiot!" screamed Satan. "Where in hell have you been? We've been using drugs in the US for years. How do you think we've destroyed so many families and the lives of all those kids?"

Another demon suggested alcohol. Satan wasn't impressed, pointing out that alcohol had already captured the hearts of countless individuals. The havoc wreaked upon innocent lives by drunken drivers had given evil many victories in the past.

"What about sexual promiscuity and perversion?" suggested one lieutenant. "It worked with Sodom and it worked with Rome!"

"Are you out of your flaming mind?" shouted Lucifer. "How do you think I created AIDS and the dissolution of so many marriages? These have been two of our greatest successes over these weak-minded humans. But this isn't nearly enough. We must come up with something that will topple the nation. Something that will thoroughly disgust God and cause Him to remove His favor from them as a people."

"War!" screamed the archdemon. "War always works, no matter who it is. Remember how we almost stopped the United States in its tracks by getting relatives and Christians to kill each other in that, what was it called, uncivil war?"

"Civil War! Civil War, you numbskull!!" corrected Satan. "We have kept wars alive for millennia. Look at the success we've had with the Semites killing each other all these centuries. I've got to hand it to you, at least you're beginning to think." Hatred and greed and several other ideas were proposed and discussed until finally a chief demon, who had been quiet all the while, made his suggestion.

"I think I've got it, Boss! By George, I think I've got it," he began deliberately. "Let's tempt the people into killing babies. Remember how we got King Herod to engage in infanticide? We almost succeeded in stopping Jesus in his tracks before he could even grow into manhood. And remember how successful we were with Pharaoh in getting him to kill all those babies in an attempt to snuff out the disgusting life of Moses?"

"But those were individual madmen who were on our side from the beginning. The trick is, how can we get an entire civilized and cultured nation to start killing babies?" challenged Satan.

"By giving the baby killing a name that will make it seem like it's a noble and worthy cause. By convincing selfish people that they really don't have the time or financial resources to raise children," he explained.

"What kind of name do you have in mind?" demanded Satan.

"Well, remember how we have always used euphemisms to cover up the nastiness and ugliness of sin? I mean, we used the term 'affair' to identify adultery. People just love that. And we used 'alternate lifestyle' to make people comfortable with sodomy and perversion. We even used 'stretching the truth' so those idiots would feel more comfortable telling lies."

"Okay, okay! You've made your point," shouted Satan impatiently. "Now what in Hades could we possibly call the murdering of babies that would fool even the stupid ones living in America?"

"Well, we could have them call it something like 'planned parenting' or maybe 'choice'," suggested the evil spirit.

"Yes! That's it! Brilliant!" Satan gleefully shouted, echoing in the corridors of hell. The more he thought about the idea, the more he liked it.

"People are so selfish and gullible these days," he thought to himself. "Why haven't I thought of this before?"

"Boss! Know what else we could do? We could make the people who are killing babies and pretending it is a good and honorable thing to do . . . we could tempt them into doing something maniacally contradictory. We could make them cry out against the injustice of taking the life of murderers. The very ones killing the most innocent of God's creation would lobby for mercy to be granted to the most evil of adults, our most devoted disciples. Just think of it. No capital punishment. Murdering those innocent little unborn babies and letting the dregs of society go unpunished. God would surely destroy a nation like that."

After more discussion, the meeting adjourned with the challenge to all demons present to implement this new program of infanticide. The code name for it was unanimous: "Choice." It was also agreed that if politicians and the courts got their noses involved, it would be much easier to achieve. A rose by any other name. Satan had come to the conclusion that if he could get a nation as great as the United States of America to diminish the value of human life, he could accomplish almost anything.

And he smugly said to himself, "And I thought Hitler's genocide of the Jews was my greatest triumph. Humph! This new program will make that look like child's play." The demons chuckled.

Suddenly I awoke from my slumber trembling, sweating. Was this merely a dream? Surely such a terrible tragedy could never happen to enlightened people. Not in the land of the free and the home of the brave. Not with citizens who have "In God We Trust" emblazoned on their currency.

"Undoubtedly this was only a terribly fiendish vision of the night," I thought to myself. Yet, it all seemed so real.

A Quick Business Call

"Honey, I think I'll call our mortgage company to see why our curtailment wasn't listed on our last statement."
Dial.
Ring.
"Hello! This is We Really Care Mortgage. If you have a touch tone-phone, press 1 now."
Press.
Ring . . . Ring . . . Ring . . . Ring . . . Ring . . . Ring . . . Ring . . . Ring . . . Ring . . . Ring . . .
"Hello. If you have a question about your interest rate, press 1. If you forgot your account number, press 2. If you are late with your monthly payment, press 911. If you have lost your statement, press 3. If you wish to refinance, press 4. If you are angry at us for having a computer generated menu like this, press *#*##. If you wish to speak to a live customer service agent, press 0."
Press.
Ring . . . Ring . . .
"Hello. I'm not at my desk at the present time, but if you'd like to leave any voice mail, you may do so at the tone."
Tone.
"Hey! This is Cletis Cratchet. Did you ever receive my $50,000 in twenties I sent last week? Call me back when you can. No need to hurry. No biggie!"
Click.
"Sweetheart, I can't believe that mortgage company! I was on the phone half an hour and didn't speak to a living soul. I'm going to try one more time and punch in one of those earlier numbers. Surely I can talk to a breathing human being."
"Darling, don't call me 'Shirley.'"
Dial.

Ring.

"Hello! This is We Really Care Mortgage. If you have a Touch-Tone phone, please press 1 now."

Press.

Ring . . . Ring . . . Ring . . . Ring . . . Ring . . . Ring . . . Ring . . . Ring . . . Ring (83 more times)

"Hello. If you have a . . . ."

Press.

Ring.

"Hi! This is Barbara. Do you have a question about your interest rate?"

"No, Barbara. I have a question about my curtailment."

"Sir, that's a different department. I'll just transfer your call directly."

"No! Wait!! Please don't do . . . ."

". . . Silver Bells, it's Christmas time in the city. Ring-a-ling. Here them ring. Soon it will be . . . ."

"Curtailment department. We are out to lunch right now. Office hours are from 9 to 5 Pacific time weekdays except holidays. Our customers always come first. Thanks so much for allowing us the privilege of being of service to you. Please call again any time. And always remember, we care."

Dial tone.

"Honey, it's late. What's for supper?"

"Dear, I thought you were going to wash the car."

"Oh, I was. But that was this morning, before I called the mortgage company. Hey, I'm hungry."

"Military Time?"

Taking my car to the garage for warranty work and service is always a hassle for me, as I'm sure it is for most people. Sadly, a few greedy mechanics have made a bad name for the rest of those honest men and women who keep our wheels running. I've had my share of encounters with service people whom I knew were lying simply because their lips were moving.

"Sir, it will take about $900 to get your car purring again."

I'm tempted to ask, "Really, then how much would you charge me to just get it to 'meow' for a while?"

Anyway, here I am again, sitting in the service department waiting room wondering why I am here. I mean, it's not like I have an antique I'm trying to keep on the road. I don't even have an "older" late model. I have a current year model that is still under warranty and I find myself more and more in the need of car service. And it's not that the car is necessarily engineered wrong or put together sloppily. At least I don't think that's the case. It's that the morons running service departments must have been trained at some deli in Hackensack.

Let me explain. Today I'm here to get a seat belt replaced that doesn't really need replacing. "How can that be?" you are asking yourself. It seems I purchased a car with carpeting cut too short in width at the factory to cover the floor without coming out from the side panels. So, I had to schedule a service time for the carpet replacement. After reinstalling new carpet, the certified mechanics (certifiable is more like it) reinstalled my front seat belts improperly. They wouldn't unfurl (the seat belts, I mean). So I scheduled another service time for them to "adjust" the belts. Guess what? They adjusted them all right. But they also ordered another seat belt for the driver's side which I didn't need after they adjusted both belts. While they were fixing the belts they ordered an extra belt, just in case. Now they are telling me they must put on the seat belt even though I don't need it, because they can't return it. I suspect it has something to do with "not wanting to return it" and also not getting paid their warranty time from the manufacturer.

I lied. I'm not really here to get my seat belt replaced. I figured that if I didn't need service, I wasn't going to put myself in harm's way for nothing. It's bad enough to get service and end up getting home to find out something else is wrong. The seat belts were messed up while they were doing carpet replacement, remember? Now, what I'm really here for is that the last time I was here was because after the seat belt adjustment, my horn wouldn't work, my cruise control wouldn't work and the airbag light kept flashing intermittently. So, of course, I scheduled another visit with the dealership to have these things fixed. When I got home, sure enough, the horn worked, the cruise control was functioning properly and the airbag light was no longer flashing. You would think that would be enough to make a new car owner proud. Wrong. When I got home, my digital clock was registering "military" time. Can you believe it? I mean, instead of 3:00 p.m. showing digitally, it would register 15:00 hours. Now I don't know about anyone else, but the closest I got to the military was ROTC in college. And, frankly, I didn't enjoy standing in the hot sun and humidity in those ugly itchy green wool winter suits they issued to college kids. So, you can imagine how much I enjoy translating military time into "civilian" time while cruising down the highway. So, yes, here I sit awaiting someone to find out why my clock has joined the army all of a sudden.

Before the carpet problem, I had brought my car to the dealership to have my fuel access door adjusted. It wouldn't open from its remote release beside the driver's seat. Push as I may, that little side door wouldn't open. So, every time I got gas, I had to open my trunk and reach in and use the manual release on the gas access door. This got to be a pain in the neck, especially when the trunk release remote next to the driver's seat quit functioning as well. I had to start the gassing process by getting out of the car, opening my trunk with the key, manually pulling the open cord for the gas access door and then pump gas. I should have known better than to have those things "fixed."

Before the gas cover problem my seat belt light would remain on in spite of my having my seat belt on. I went to have that fixed, a "simple adjustment" the service writer said, only to get home and find my light warning buzzer stuck on buzz all the while I was driving. I actually started to think my car was possessed. I even thought of having it "repossessed," if you know what I mean.

Before the control panel problems, I discovered a rattle in the truck of the car that was annoying, but not life-threatening. I drove with the rattle for a month before deciding I couldn't take it any more. I should have slept in that day. Not only did they not find the source of the rattle, but they caused two more problems to develop. The remote mirror control quit working and the glove box cover kept falling down into my wife's lap. We were still enjoying the new car smell when all of this started to happen. And it's strange. It's strange because if you wash my car and park it outside our house, it is quite an impressive looking piece of transportation equipment. It is stylish. It is sleek and aerodynamic. Nobody would even dare to suspect it was a piece of inoperative junk.

Before the last enumerated problems, I had taken it to the dealership because of a clicking sound under the hood. I thought it sounded like a fan hitting some plastic. But the mechanic swore it was a transmission problem. I hated to hear that because every time some mechanic got into the "guts" of one of my past cars, they always leaked after that (the cars, I mean). I just knew that if he broke seals and invaded the viscera of my transmission I would have a dirty concrete slab for a garage floor. It was prophetic. I do.

Before that I had first approached the dealership to point out that I didn't have my spare "donut" tire in the trunk of the car. With the suspicious looks they gave me, you would have thought they thought I had stolen it and sold it on the black market. Not only was my spare missing, but my floor mats that were supposed to come with the model were nowhere to be found. The way I figure it, I would be way ahead in time and frustration had I bought my own spare and paid for a set of floor mats.

I have a theory about all of this. I think there is a guy (or maybe a gal) trained by car dealerships to put curses on the cars that come to them for service. Yes. I mean, think about it. How many people do you know that have had what I have detailed here, or worse, happen to them? Did you ever hear of someone purchasing a car with a 36,000 mile warranty that didn't have to go back and forth numerous times to have things fixed? This alone proves my theory to be correct. There is someone at dealerships trained and skilled in the voodoo arts of witchcraft and hexes. My poor little car has had enough hexes on it for a lifetime of ten cars. It's a wonder it even starts when I go to drive it each day. I even hated to mention that for fear that is the next hex. At least all of the things wrong with my car allowed me to still be able to drive it to the dealer.

I don't know where he is, or where she may sit. But there is a highly paid employee at car dealerships whose duty it is to make things go wrong with brand new cars in order for the dealer to make all that money from the manufacturer on warranty work. And I'll bet you a new seat belt it's the awful truth!

Maxims Revisited

Did you ever have the urge to challenge one of those erudite sages who always seemed to have an appropriate one liner? Glib maxims of absolute truth seem to roll off their tongues like honey from the comb. Oh, the pain! But who in his right mind wants to impugn beliefs that have been so often repeated they seem etched in granite? Okay, so maybe I'm not in my right mind. Here are a few of those propositions assumed to be true, with no corroborating proof:

There are no ugly people. Have you looked in the mirror lately? Just kidding. If by ugly one means that all humans are created in God's image and God doesn't make junk—correct. But Satan has made a lot of folks ugly with sin.

There are no stupid questions, only stupid answers. Now isn't that stupid? I've heard stupid questions all my life. Questions like, "Didn't the universe come about merely by chance?" Or maybe one like, "The Bible doesn't say I **can't** do it, does it?" Here's a good one. "Would you like to help me haul garbage to the dump in your new car?" Stupid!

Cleanliness is next to godliness. Not necessarily. It's more like "cleanliness is next to impossible." I've met some pretty dirty fellows who looked mighty holy to me. John the Baptist was hardly the best groomed circuit rider of his day. Disciples of Jesus are eager to get their hands soiled in service to the Master.

Early to bed and early to rise makes a young man healthy, wealthy, and wise. It ain't necessarily so. I read of an illiterate who keeps miserable hours yet won the lottery. The outcome of one's life depends upon what he does during his waking hours, no matter what the time of day.

Never look a gift horse in the mouth. Why not? It depends on what the gift is. Is it money to buy your vote? Is it bribery to secure your silence? Drugs? Sex? Satan can wrap some pretty sorry looking nags in paper and bows and fool us. Shouldn't someone have looked more closely at that Trojan horse?

If at first you don't succeed, try, try again. Perhaps other doors of service are being made available. Maybe you are forcing something you aren't suited for. Even the apostles had failures and went elsewhere.

A bird in the hand is worth two in the bush. Depends upon whose bush and what kind of bird. Often the things we have are not what we need/want most. Occasionally we settle for coach when first class has already been provided.

Two's company, three's a crowd. In romance, perhaps, but not in the family of God. The more the merrier. The harmony of three is preferred to the duet. I like the preacher who, when asked how many more members the church needed, always answered, "One more!"

Lightning never strikes the same place twice. Better talk to Gunston Skomedal about that. He was struck nine times. Was he standing in the same spot? Who knows. But oddsmakers will be able to tell you when lighting might strike him again.

It's always darkest before the dawn. What if you live in Alaska — the Land of the Midnight Sun? What if it's Monday Night Football? Absolutes aren't always so absolute.

Money is the root of all evil. First, get it right. Its the *love* of money that's the root of *all kinds* of evil. Money isn't evil in and of itself. It's merely a medium of exchange. But evil minds find it increasingly easy to put money before people and profit before principles.

There is more than one fish in the sea. True, but we won't be able to meet all those other fish. So, we had better treat people right and not be so eager to toss friendships back into the ocean.

The grass is always greener on the other side of the hill. Flat not so! I looked. And that green stuff wasn't even grass. It was weeds. And it still had to be mowed. And it was over a septic tank. So learn to take care of your own back yard.

It's not whether you win or lose that matters, but how you play the game. Oh, yeah? Vince Lombardi asked, "If that's true, then why does someone always keep score?" It does matter if you win or lose. All God's children can be winners!

Don't judge someone until you've walked a mile in his shoes. What if his shoes don't fit? Besides, we aren't given the prerogative to judge others even after we've traveled in their footwear. That's the Lord's business.

Act your age. Why? Why fit into preconceived stereotypes? Act as young as you feel. Go ahead! It's not illegal.

Better safe than sorry. Tell Sergeant York that. And George Washington. Playing it safe is the coward's way. Jesus didn't play it safe. Neither did Paul. Heroes take chances. Bravery is born of risk.

A dog is man's best friend. Some cat aficionados would disagree. Soul mates know better.

Every little bit helps. Sometimes a "little bit" isn't enough. Little bits can signify selfish hearts and stingy minds. Settling on the little may keep us from occasionally doing a lot.

All's fair in love and war. Nope! Rules don't change simply because circumstances do. Integrity must thrive in all climates. Wars don't negate morality. A lie is still a lie regardless of whether we are loving or fighting.

Never say never. Why not? Who wants a mate who says, "Hardly ever." To declare "never" involved the desire to keep one's word. Do we serve a God who promises "rarely" to desert us?

You can't judge a book by its cover. Sure you can! Trash is usually wrapped in trash. One's dress and countenance can have a direct correlation to what he really is on the inside. Winners don't typically dress like losers. And vice versa.

A fool and his money are soon parted. Nada! Some fools keep their wealth right up to dispatching time. Remember the man who tore down his barns and built bigger ones? Being able to manage money doesn't guarantee escape from fooldom. Consider Howard Hughes.

Better late than never. Why be late in the first place? Some people seem to delight in the fact that they are generally not dependable when it comes to punctuality, unless maybe it involves their jobs. Do you suppose anyone will be late for judgment day?

Pretty is as pretty does. Hypocrisy always wears a façade. Satan appears as an angel of light.

Don't cry over spilled milk. It's okay to weep over mistakes, so long as we learn from them.

Practice what you preach. Why not preach what you practice? Be truthful. Let others know how you truly feel, then behave accordingly. Preaching what we practice might change behavior for the better.

Where there's a will there's a way. I've personally had plenty of *will* when there was even more *won't*. Desire isn't enough. Reality occasionally forces us to admit, "No way!"

You can't teach an old dog new tricks. Sure you can. And old folks, too. Some of our greatest literature and inventions and music came from the minds of creative people past fifty. Retirees are retooling their minds for a second time around. Hooray!

Dead men don't tell tales. Don't tell archaeologists this. They'll laugh. Ever read any O. Henry recently? Shakespeare? Zane Gray? Louis L'Amour? Matthew? Mark? Luke? John? The Bible affirms that Abel's blood cries to us from the grave.

People who live in glass houses shouldn't throw stones. Okay, I'll concede this one. But they ought to at least keep their drapes closed.

Losing My Neck

A local department store was offering a special on picture portraits in their photography studio. I needed a business photo for a book dust jacket and, being Scotch and all, didn't feel the desire to pay a photographer $500 for a lousy mug shot. Somewhere along the line I discovered I had lost my neck. I'm still barely recovered from the shock to recall the account accurately. But let me start at the beginning.

Me: "Hi! Do you have a special on portraits?"
Her (giving me her brochure that announced 90 portraits for $4.95): "We sure do!"
Me: "Wow! How can you take 90 different poses and stay in business? I mean, the cost of the film alone would wipe you out!"
Her: "They are only copies."
Me: "Beg pardon?"
Her: "It's 90 copies of the same pose."
Me: "Oh, I see. You mean you will only take one pose and I have to like that one?"
Her: "No, sir. I'll take several poses and let you look at each one on the screen. Then you pick your favorite pose and we make 90 pictures of that one sitting."

At this point I was beginning to think there was a tooth fairy. "What a bargain," I thought to myself. There must be some catch. That's too cheap for 90 copies. My goodness, whatever would I do with 90 pictures of myself anyway? That would allow one picture for every fan club of mine with 89 left over. After all, I'm not a kid anymore. I can't send a wallet-size snapshot of myself to all my uncles and aunts and every second cousin. They'd think I was crazy. I could give my father one. That would leave 88. Then I would send one for the book to the publisher. Let's see now. That would leave 87. What am I going to do with 87 pictures of myself? Things like this have to be thought through carefully. One doesn't want to waste $4.95 on just any get-rich-quick scheme that comes along. One can't be too careful these days.

Me: "What's the catch?"

Her: "What do you mean?"

Me: "There has to be some fine print that says, 'Camera rental $200' and 'flash bulb depreciation $10' or something like that."

Her: "Oh, no, sir! The pictures are only $4.95. It's quite a bargain."

Me: "Okay! Let's do it."

Her: "Please sign this form stating that I've explained the program to you. Also, notice the $25 sitting fee."

Me: "What did you say?"

Her: "There is a flat sitting fee of $25 for every customer we photograph."

Me: "What's a sitting fee?"

Her: "It's for the overall cost of sitting and posing in our studio."

I just knew it. I knew there was a built-in expense somewhere. Nobody could offer 90 pictures for $4.95 unless the photographs were so tiny you'd need a magnifying glass to see them.

Me: "Why don't you folks just tell the truth up front?"

Her: "Excuse me?"

Me: "I mean, why lure some poor soul into your studio under the pretense of 90 pictures for $4.95? Why not just tell us it will cost $30 for the offer?"

Her: "Sir, I just work here. I don't make the rules."

I was upset enough to leave, but I needed the snapshot so desperately and my little town didn't have one of those booths where you sit and grin into a mirror and get 4 different poses for $2. Now that's a bargain! But, $30 for one pose 90 times? I don't think so.

Her (sensing my hesitation): "Well, do you want your picture taken or not?" She certainly hadn't taken any Dale Carnegie courses.

Me: "Did you say the $25 was a sitting fee?"

Her: "That's right!"

Me: "Take my picture with me standing. I don't need to sit to
  have a head shot, do I? Just wave the sitting fee if you will."
Her (smirking a bit this time): "Look, it doesn't work that way.
  What'll it be?"
Me: "Oh, all right. Go ahead. But I hope you tell your boss I
  said to post the cost up front instead of hiding it in some
  so-called 'sitting fee.' That's almost false advertising."
Her: "I'll be sure to tell him."

I was soon to discover I had lost my neck. Not my shirt,
mind you. I could afford the $30. The well-trained photogra-
pher had me turn my head this way and turn my head that
way. She had me gaze at an imaginary dot on the wall. You'd
think for $30 a pop they'd be able to afford a real dot. Be that
as it may, and I try my very best at such times as this to avoid
clichés like the plague, she finally came up with several poses
from which I could choose my favorite.

Over the years I have put on a few pounds on this once
140 pound frame. When my family snapshot was taken for
the church picture board recently, I did notice that I looked a
little "too tucked in" or something. The picture reminded me
of a turtle who had just eaten and couldn't get his head all the
way into his shell. Little did I know that all the pizza and
burgers and rutabaga sandwiches (my wife is vegetarian)
would take their ultimate toll on my physique.

Her: "How do you like these poses?"
Me: "Where are *my* poses?"
Her: "These *are* your poses, sir!"
Me: "Is that the best you can do?"
Her: "Sir, the camera takes what it sees."

The poses were horrible. "Do I look like this in the pulpit
on Sundays?" I thought to myself. I looked like a cross
between a Neanderthal and Fred Flintstone.

Me: "Where is my neck?" I bellowed, without realizing it.
Her: "Excuse me?"
Me: "Oh, never mind."
Her: "These are very good, aren't they? This one here is espe-
  cially your likeness."

You've got to be kidding. I can't look like that. When did I lose my neck? Why didn't someone tell me? Why wasn't I warned this could happen? I look like a guy at a baseball game who's just been yelled at, "Heads up!" after a foul ball. You know the look. Every one loses their necks for a few seconds. But this was different. My neck had disappeared permanently. This is outrageous. And the worst part was that I was committed to the girl for $30.

Let's see. I could put these snapshots in my garden. No rabbit or insects or birds would dare think twice about approaching. After making my "best pose" selection, I made a hasty retreat. Just outside the little studio was a big display of some new diet drink. "Why put your diet section right outside a picture studio?" I asked myself. Before the thought had filtered completely through, it dawned on me. Dummy! One look at your "best pose" ought to answer that in spades.

May Day - May Day
Dear Publisher:
    I haven't any recent snapshots of myself that would be worthy of a jacket cover. Please go ahead and do the cover without my image. I'd hate to do anything to adversely harm the marketing of our book.
                    Sincerely,

                    Barney Rubble

About the Illustrator

Gary W. Royse was born in Coffeyville, Kansas in 1956. While attending college in Pratt, Kansas to study for the Fish and Game Service, Gary displayed a watercolor painting of antelope. Response was overwhelming enough to convince Gary to change his major from Fish and Game to Commercial Illustration and to transfer 200 miles to another college.

Gary received his AA degree in commercial illustration from Labette Community College and has done freelance art ever since. His chief influences have been his instructor, Ted Watts, nationally known sports artist, Keith Birdsong, and Carl Brenders. His wife, Sherry, is also an aspiring artist.

He has prints, commissioned drawings of wildlife, and portraits scattered from Kansas City to Texas. Gary has over fourteen prints available for purchase and can be consulted directly for commissioned artwork. You may contact Gary at his address: 7254 Beef Branch Road, Joplin, MO 64804. Or, by phone: (417) 623-1342.

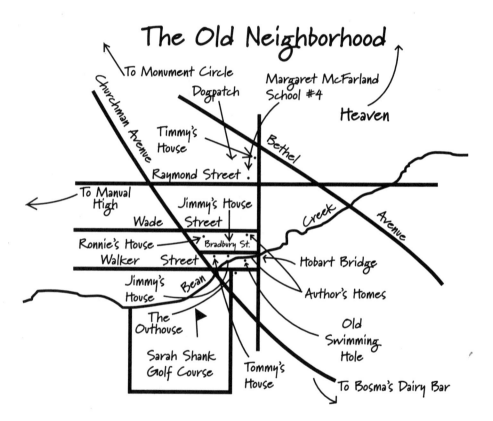

The Old Neighborhood

To Monument Circle

Dogpatch

Margaret McFarland
School #4

Heaven

Churchman Avenue

Timmy's
House

Bethel

Raymond Street

To Manual
High

Jimmy's House

Creek

Avenue

Wade   Street

Ronnie's House

Bradbury St.

Walker   Street

Hobart Bridge

Jimmy's
House

Bean

Author's Homes

The
Outhouse

Old
Swimming
Hole

Sarah Shank
Golf Course

Tommy's
House

To Bosma's Dairy Bar